Startup

the complete handbook
for launching a company for less

Startup

the complete handbook
for launching a company for less

Elizabeth Edwards

Essential Books
Cincinnati

Published in the United States by Essential Books.

Startup: The Complete Handbook for Launching a Company for Less is a trademark of Elizabeth Edwards.

Sincere thanks to Intuit, Matthew Kelly, eBay, Skype, eHealthInsurance, Google, RetailMeNot.com, Priceline, Bed&Breakfast Online, Springwise, Money Magazine, Parker Brothers, Osterwader et al, Jim Muehlhausen, Chris Anderson, Timothy Ferriss, Clayton Christensen, Hoovers, the US Census Bureau, Alexa, CrunchBase, SurveyMonkey, Zillow, LendingClub, the Angel Capital Association, SCORE, Entrepreneur.com, SBIR.gov, Foundation Center, Grants.gov, the OnCycle team at UC DAAP, USPTO.gov, WhoIs.com, Nivea, L'Oreal, BlendTec, DaFont.com, iStockPhoto, CrowdSpring, Behance.net, PRWeb, Apple, GEICO, Chick-Fil-A, Facebook, Jigsaw, Etsy, MailChimp, RedBull, HubSpot, YouTube, David Meerman Scott, LinkedIn, Twitter, ShareThis, Salesforce.com, Procter & Gamble, BaseCamp, GoDaddy, Shopify, LoopNet, Insurance Edge and Sequoia Capital for being great resources for entrepreneurs and for allowing me to use their name and images.

Edwards, Elizabeth A.
Startup: The Complete Handbook for Launching a Company for Less

ISBN: 9780983208617
1. Business planning. 2. New business enterprises. 3. Entrepreneurship.

Library of Congress Control Number 2010942449

Also available in hardcover and as an eBook.

Essential Books
PO Box 9563
Cincinnati, Ohio 45209-9998

www.elizabethedwards.com

For Mom

Thanks for always being my cheerleader.

Table of Contents

Introduction

Entrepreneurship is a noble pursuit – a right and a privilege passed down to us by the founding fathers, who imagined a country where any person could pursue their dream and make their fortune.

I've found that there are two categories of books on entrepreneurship: business plan workbooks that have a lot of empty charts and offer little in the way of advice and 'get rich quick' books that tell the story of an extremely lucky entrepreneur, but offer very few details as to how they did it.

Most of the business books that I read today focus on high-level strategy, but rarely get down to brass tacks: how much things cost, how to do things better – and which services to use.

There are a lot of books about startups that talk about how to make it big, but few that spend any time outlining how to not go bankrupt in 12 months. See, entrepreneurship is just as much about survival as it is about wealth. So half of this book is focused on saving money and mitigating risk. I've seen too many startups begin their journey with big dreams, only to get billed to death before they've even made a sale.

I have been very lucky to participate in the building of several successful startups and work with some of the brightest financial and legal minds in venture capital – and some of the world's foremost branding and design firms. I've taken the best of those experiences and written them down here – so that you can benefit from them as well.

This book is based on my personal experiences funding startups as a venture capital investor, serving on the advisory boards of startups, and starting my own company a little more than a year ago.

All of the strategies, tactics, and calculations that I outline in this book are ones that I have used successfully myself. Each of the products and services I recommend are ones that I have researched extensively, bought, and use today.

This book is not just for the budding technology mogul who plans to raise venture capital – it's also for the freelance designer, the landscaper, and the coffee shop owner who plans to apply for an SBA loan. Businesses of all kinds need the same things in order to be successful:
-   a business model that is designed to be profitable
-   a value proposition that customers want
-   a brand that people like and remember
-   a marketing and PR strategy that effectively gets the word out
-   back office operations that run smoothly and inexpensively
-   a legal structure, policies, insurance, and IP filings that protect your assets and your company's assets

We will tackle all of these components – and look for ways to conserve cash, get operational fast, and get the best for less.

Entrepreneurship is not for everyone. But if it's for you, then I know this book will help you get there faster, save you a lot of time, and a lot of money.

You'll be amazed at what you can accomplish. Good luck.

Yours truly,

Elizabeth Edwards

Summary of the $100,000 in savings in this book

	Cost description	Average startup	With this handbook	Total Savings
Branding & Design	Branding Logo & Other Design	$20,000 $10,000	$0 $1,000	$20,000 $9,000
Marketing	Publicity SEO Advertising	$5,000 $2,000 $7,000	$500 $0 $2,000	$4,500 $2,000 $5,000
Admin	Website Phone/Voicemail Email Project Mgmt Accounting & Tax	$6,000 $2,400 $1,000 $500 $5,000	$1,000 $0 $0 $0 $500	$5,000 $2,400 $1,000 $500 $4,500
Legal	Incorporating Copyright Trademark Provisional Patent	$2,000 $235 $1,325 $3,150	$100 $35 $325 $150	$1,900 $200 $1,000 $3,000
	Total startup cost savings	$65,610	$5,610	$60,000
Personal financial makeover	Personal budget Credit score savings & savings on purchases			$20,000 $20,000
	Total startup and personal savings			$100,000

1   The Pros & Cons of Entrepreneurship

About 90% of business knowledge is a series of templates. Sales projections, contracts, terms and conditions, project plans, logos and taglines, business plans, financial models, press releases, and on and on. The other 10% is the creative: what you're going to do differently. Maybe it's your service delivery. Maybe it's your brand – or your technology or your company culture. But in this book, we're going to tackle the 90% of the costs, time, and work required to launch your company and we're going to show you how to do it cheaper, faster, and better.

The cost of starting a business has radically decreased over the last decade. In 2000, the average cost to launch a technology startup was $1,000,000. Today, it's about $50,000. And following the plan in this book, you'll be able to start up for *even less.*

We'll use new technologies - such as cloud hosting, variable print technology, mass customization, long-tail distribution, crowdsourcing, online templates, and hundreds of new online services - to dramatically decrease the cost of starting a business.

The purpose of this book is to really paint a picture for you of what being an entrepreneur means so that you can enter the world of entrepreneurship with both eyes open and increase your chances of success. We'll look at historical statistics on entrepreneurs, examine the strategies of successful startups, and sift through some of the failures. We'll evaluate the costs, the odds of success, the benefits, and the risks. And most importantly – considering all of these, we'll recommend the best approach.

So let's start off with the most important question: **Does it pay to be an entrepreneur?** It's important to understand the benefits of being an entrepreneur as well as understanding the risk.

Short-term sacrifice, long-term wealth & flexibility

Probably the two biggest benefits of entrepreneurship are ownership (wealth) and control. Established entrepreneurs enjoy more flexibility in their schedule than their employed peers – leading to more overall satisfaction. In the U.S., 62.5% of entrepreneurs report that they are satisfied or very satisfied with their work, compared with 45.9% of people who work for others.

The business case for entrepreneurship and its wealth-creating benefits has been quantified by the Survey of Consumer Finances. It turns out that entrepreneurs (classified as self employed) report both a greater income and much greater net worth than their peers who work for someone else.

In 2007, the average net worth (assets minus liabilities) for a self-employed household was $2,000,000 - nearly six times greater than their employed peers, whose average net worth was $350,000. The difference in net worth is mostly tied to the difference in average income: Self-employed households had an average income more than double that of those who work for others - $191,000 vs. $83,100.

This means that entrepreneurs are not only happier because of their increased flexibility and control; they are also wealthier.

Wealth Distribution of
Employees and Entrepreneurs

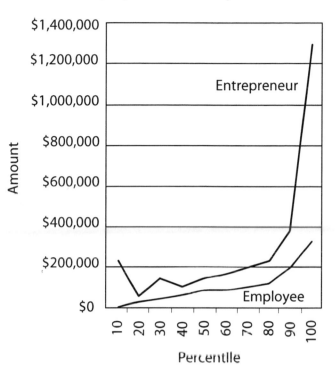

Source: Scott A. Shane (adapted from V. Quadrini)

The First Two Years: Ramen Noodles & Long Hours

Over 530,000 new businesses are created each month in the U.S. There are many good reasons to become an entrepreneur: You get to choose your own hours, work a flexible schedule and have your own independence. But you should equally consider the pros and cons of entrepreneurship before quitting your job and investing all of your time and money into a great idea.

Do not become an entrepreneur if you want to get rich quick. Great businesses take 10 years to grow up and most lose money in the first few years. Coupled with the hours you will be putting in, it's quite likely you will be making less than minimum wage for the first few years at least. On average, entrepreneurs make $30,000-$40,000 in the first few years – just enough to survive. It's only when the business is established that the fat salaries, tax write offs, and entrepreneurial perks kick in.

Typically, in the first year, you're on your own. Only 21% of new businesses hire someone else in the first year - which means that you're now in charge of sales, business development, new product development, marketing, advertising, accounting, administrative duties – and you'll likely be working more hours than ever before.

Business owners work on average **10%-30%** longer than their employed peers. Your 40-hour week may look more like **45-55** hours per week – or more. And if you're working 80 hours a week, you don't have a lot of opportunity for flexible hours since you're working every waking minute.

Only once the business is established can an entrepreneur enjoy flexible hours. In the first few years, there's not enough downtime for flexibility.

Rational & Irrational Risk Factors for Startups

According to the SBA, over **50% of small businesses fail in the first five years**. Now, these numbers are slightly inflated because most of these "failures" are voluntary closings – not bankruptcies. But regardless, most businesses do not make it to year five.

These figures aren't meant to scare you, but to prepare you for the rocky path ahead. Underestimating risk is one of the biggest obstacles entrepreneurs face.

Rational risks

So let's examine why these businesses fail. There are rational reasons – and in his book *Small Business Management*, Michael Ames gives the following reasons for small business failure:

1. Lack of experience
2. Insufficient capital (money)
3. Poor location
4. Poor inventory management
5. Over-investment in fixed assets
6. Poor credit arrangements
7. Personal use of business funds
8. Unexpected growth
9. Competition
10. Low sales

Irrational Risk Aversion

So even considering all these rational risks and pitfalls of entrepreneurship – at the end of the day, if you're a top performer and you're willing to work hard on a good opportunity, you're better off as an entrepreneur.

So what holds us back? Irrational Risk Aversion. Risk aversion basically means that we don't like losing our stuff. So, in order to avoid that unpleasant feeling of loss (or temporary sacrifice), we consistently settle for less overall. Even when we stand to create *six times more wealth* in the long term by starting our own company, we prefer that consistent paycheck today from our employer.

The interesting thing is that risk aversion is not rational – it's emotional! It doesn't make mathematical sense.

Economists did a study with capuchin monkeys and they taught them how to use currency. So immediately, the monkeys formed a market for prostitution (typical!). But even more interestingly, they showed a measurable aversion to risk that's identical to day traders in the stock market. That's right: our aversion to risk goes back to our primate roots – it's hardwired into our DNA.

So, if there's one thing I'd like you to take away from this book, it's this: Don't be a monkey. Run the numbers and make a rational decision. Otherwise, your genetic preference for a steady paycheck is only going to hold you back in the long run.

We're going to arm you with rational tools for financial calculations, concept evaluation, risk mitigation, and resources that will help you take a calculated risk. We'll pursue cost-saving strategies to reduce your overall exposure to risk and make sure you run the numbers before making any big decisions.

Life Plan before Business Plan

You need a plan to build a house. To build a life, it is even more important to have a plan or goal.
– Zig Ziglar

Why are you doing this? Is the business plan you're about to write going to fit in with your *life*? One of the best life-goals frameworks was developed by Matthew Kelley, author of The *Rhythm of Life* and *The Dream Manager*. It's summarized in chart form on the next page.

Kelly's life plan and goal setting system uses 13 different elements of our lives (financial, creative, professional, etc) and three different time horizons (12 months, 1-5 years, and 5 years and beyond) to help define the scope of life goals.

Go through the exercise of writing down your goals — and make sure that entrepreneurship fits within the overall plan. Try to list at least 2-3 goals in each cell - from the big and exciting to the small and mundane.

	12 months	1-5 years	5 years+
Physical			
Mental			
Emotional			
Spiritual			
Psychological			
Material			
Financial			
Adventure			
Creative			
Intellectual			
Professional			
Legacy			
Character			

2   Startup Finance is Personal Finance

"Never spend your money before you have it."
– Thomas Jefferson

Whether you can start your own business is going to be partially dependent on your personal financial situation – how stable your finances currently are. So let's get a handle on your personal finances first.

Why you want to be an entrepreneur is really a much deeper question. But it's one worth asking before you spend a single dime. Being an entrepreneur is going to have a big impact on your lifestyle. In the short run, you're going to work longer hours and make less money. On average, in the long run, you'll be wealthier and have more flexibility. Let's make sure that your business plan fits in with your overall life plan.

Get a Handle on Your Finances

Startup finance is personal finance. Regardless of how brilliant your idea is or how well written your business plan is, your personal financial stability is a function of your personal balance sheet (how much you have) and your burn rate (how much you spend each year). Your access to outside sources of capital such as banks and investors is all driven off the brilliance of your business plan, your personal balance sheet (assets and liabilities), your credit score, and, in the case of investors, your network.

The following four factors – your assets, your liabilities, your credit score, and your network – will determine what sources of capital are available to you, keeping in mind that your business may require either debt or equity or both.

Your assets: Your assets, such as your home, can be a form of security/leverage if you are borrowing money.
- Do you own a home? Do you have equity in your home?
- Do you have cash savings or other assets?

Your liabilities: If you already have a high debt-to-equity ratio (a lot of liabilities), this could prevent you from borrowing more capital.
- Do you have credit card or other debt?
- Do you have other fixed payments, such as car payments?

Your credit score: (from the bank's perspective, your credit risk)

620 or less	High Risk – Bad Credit
660	Cut-off for many Lenders
700	Medium Risk – Good Credit
720	Medium-Low Risk – Good-Excellent Credit
740	Cut-off for many 0% credit cards
770 or up	Low Risk – Excellent Credit

Your network/access to capital: Do a quick assessment of those who are close to you and those who have significant financial capacity (making over $200,000 a year, have over $1,000,000 in assets such as property or investments).
- Your family: Would your parents, grandparents, aunts and uncles, in-laws, etc. consider backing you?

- Your friends: Would your friends or friends-of-friends consider an investment?
- Your network: Would wealthy individuals who may or may not have made money in the same field as your business consider lending financial support?

Your burn rate: A company's monthly *burn rate* is simply the monthly ongoing fixed expenses like salaries and rent. Banks and investors like to know this number because it gives them a sense for their maximum exposure.

The biggest expense for your startup in the first few years is you. That's right – your salary is going to cost your startup more than rent, web hosting, postage, shipping, or advertising. So we need to address this cost first. By reducing you personal monthly burn rate, we'll be able to reduce your startup's monthly burn rate.

So take a look at your personal monthly budget to find out how fast you burn through cash. If you can slow the burn by reducing expenses, you can conserve cash and last longer. This is really important because it may take a long while before you reach profitability. In general, it takes twice as long and costs twice as much as you think it will, so it pays to be frugal at the outset.

Determine (and monitor) your credit score for free

Credit Karma allows you to check your credit and monitor your score monthly for free.

FreeCreditReport.com is also an excellent credit reporting site, but unlike FreeCreditReport.com, Credit Karma does not require a credit card number in order to get a free credit report. If your credit is in good shape, you can stick with Credit Karma and monitor your score for free.

However, if your score isn't in the best shape, you're going to have to find out why. FreeCreditReport.com provides a much more complete report, including detailed incidents of late payments, collections, and other negative events. The report can cost anywhere from $15-30 a month, but it's worth the expense *until* you get things straightened around. The only downside is that once you get your credit straightened out and you want to cancel your subscription, you have to call their 1-800 number to cancel. Still – time and money well spent. If your score is lower than average, you need to do some work here.

Find out what incidences and factors are affecting your score and take care of any payments or disputes to **improve your score before you need to apply for credit**. If you have some outstanding issues, you're going to have to be extremely resourceful – and extremely firm – in order to get incidences removed from your report.

Credit Score

**% of Population
with that score**

Credit Score		% of Population
850		
		18%
800		
760	Best mortgage rate	19%
750		
740	Best credit card rate	
720	Best auto loan rate	16%
700		
660	Credit card approval	12%
650		
620	Mortgage approval	9%
600		
		10%
550		
		9%
500	Auto loan approval	
		7%

Source: Money Magazine

Why Credit Score Matters

Your credit score is your "risk score" to banks. Banks charge high-risk clients a risk premium – additional percentage points in interest rate – and may limit the amount of capital they lend.

Let's say you and a friend are each applying for a $50,000 loan that will be paid back over 10 years. Your friend's credit score is 800 (excellent) and your score is 600 (pretty low). The bank decides to offer your friend a 5% interest rate and offers you a 15% interest rate.

Let's look at how much your credit score affected your cost of capital (the interest rate).

- A $50,000 loan at 5% interest over 10 years costs $13,639 in interest.
- A $50,000 loan at 15% interest over 10 years costs $46,802 in interest.

You'll pay $33,000 more in interest than your friend just for being a higher risk to the bank.

Free. Estimated time to sign up: 5 minutes

Track your spending by the minute with Mint.com

Mint.com is a personal finance and accounting site that is easy to use and easy to set up. The site pulls data from your bank, brokerage, and credit card accounts  to categorize your spending, determine your outstanding balances, and the performance of your investments. It takes 30 minutes to set up and then automatically updates your account information thereafter — so you can focus on making smart decisions instead of trying to figure out where all your cash went.

Mint's best feature is its transaction categorizing technology, which uses the yellow pages to figure out where – and more importantly what type of business – you're spending money on.

So for instance, if you eat at McDonald's, you'll see a credit card transaction pop up under transactions categorized as "fast food" within the hour. This instant clarity is pretty powerful when you're trying to keep track of a lot of transactions.

When you're starting your company, you're going to want to keep track of all your business transactions when tax time rolls around since you'll write off (deduct) these expenses. The budgeting and e-mail/text alerts system is also pretty helpful when you're trying to stick to your budget. You can also tag business expenses – making it easier at tax time.

Mint is one way to keep track of your personal balance sheet:
- Cash
- Car
- House
- Investments

- Loans (car, etc)
- Credit Cards
- Mortgages

Mint is safe to use. The site uses the same layers of security that banks do to protect the data that is stored, and because Mint is a "read-only" service, you can only organize and analyze your finances, but you can't move funds between or out of your accounts.

Free. Estimated time to sign up all accounts: 30-60 minutes

Reduce your burn rate by $10,000-$ 20,000 a year

Your personal monthly burn rate – how much you need each month to live – is the number that determines how long (as in how many months) you will be able to survive while building your company. A startup is a cash hungry beast, so it helps to reduce your personal expenses before you create a monster.

Refinance your house *before* you quit your job

Refinancing your house could be your most significant area of savings. On a $250,000 mortgage, a 2% reduction in an interest rate could create up $300 a month in savings. When you consider closing costs ($1,000-$3,000), the refinancing pays for itself (in interest savings) within a year and you can typically avoid out-of-pocket costs by rolling the closing costs into the amount you refinance.

While we won't go into the moral arguments of a fixed rate vs. adjustable rate here, trust me: in the case of low rates, you want a long-term fixed-rate mortgage. Your life is going to be uncertain enough with a new business – there's no sense in throwing the monkey wrench of rising rates (and thus a quickly rising house payment) into the mix with an adjustable rate mortgage.

The rule of thumb for refinancing is this: If you can save 1% on your interest rate and you're going to be in your home for the next year or two, refinancing your home is a good use of your time. It will not only save you hundreds on your monthly payment, it will save you tens of thousands over the life of your mortgage in interest. For a great mortgage calculator, visit *www.daveramsey.com/tools/mortgage-calculator*

The only thing that would prevent you from refinancing is if your house has lost significant value – enough to be "underwater", where your outstanding balance on your loan is greater than the current market value of your home. Mint.com uses Zillow.com to update the value of your home daily, given recent property sales in your neighborhood. Zillow.com is another free resource, though its algorithm generally shows home values 10% - 20% lower than actual market values.

Credit Karma and Free Credit Report will show the outstanding balance of your mortgage on your credit report, but you can also find this information on the year-end statement your mortgage lender provides to you for tax purposes. In order to refinance your house, you're going to need roughly 20% of equity in your home.

(Home value – Outstanding Loan) / Home value = % Equity

Regardless of the result of this equation, call your lender or mortgage broker. Zillow.com only reflects the change in prices of neighboring properties, but does not reflect the improvements you have made in your home. If you updated your kitchen or bathroom, the value of your home will of course be higher, but Zillow.com has no way of knowing whether you've made any improvements. Only an appraiser can determine what your home is worth.

Refinance before you quit your job. If rates are even 1% lower, it makes sense to refinance your house, but you won't be able to refinance for at least two years once you're self-employed. That's right! Lenders like stable borrowers – and that means employment and a salary. So before you quit your job, call your lender or mortgage broker and find out how much you could save by refinancing. If you wait until you're self-employed, you're going to have to jump through a lot of hoops in order to refinance — including at least two years of solid operating history.

Total savings: $3,600-$6,000 a year, or $300-500 a month

Reduce or eliminate your car payment

Time to trade in that Mercedes — and that $600 a month car payment — for something that makes a little more sense for the next 12-24 months.

If you have a car payment, let's hope it's almost paid off. If not, you may consider switching to a cheaper ride. Your car needs to be reliable and safe, but unless it's an integral part of your business, it's just an expense — an expense that will limit your ability to borrow money for your business.

Check your balance on your car loan and you car's current Kelly Blue Book Value. If you owe a balance of $15,000 on your car and it would sell for $25,000, you can sell the car today, eliminate your car loan, and have $10,000 left over. Look for alternative used cars on eBay. Is there something serviceable that you can get for $5,000 or $10,000? If so, then it's time to trade in those wheels.

By selling your current car and buying something in the $10,000 price range, you'll eliminate that $600 a month car payment. Otherwise, that car payment is going to come back and bite you in month 10, when your sales aren't picking up quite as fast as you thought they would and you're stuck.

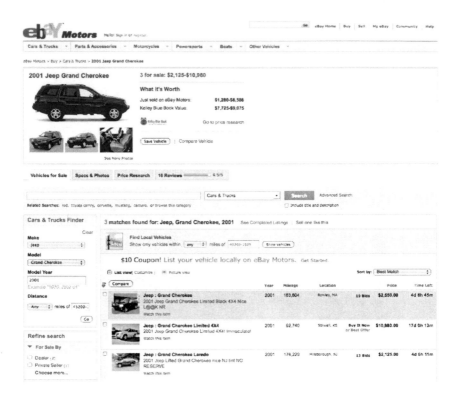

Get your car detailed, take some snazzy photos, list it on a site like eBay, and get a car you can live with for the next 12-24 months.

Total savings: $1,200-$7,200 a year, or $100-$600 a month

Start over with phone, Internet, cable, etc.

Believe me – you're not going to be watching too much TV over the next 12 months, so look for ways to cut out some of these expenses. Just by cutting cable and signing up for the minimum $8.99 a month Netflix Unlimited Streaming Video with your broadband connection and a $79 Roku box, you'll save $50-$100 a month. That's $600-$1,200 a year.

If you're like many people today, you may be using your cell phone as your only phone, meaning that you probably have one of the most expensive wireless plans. One way to cut down on your wireless minutes at home is to use a Wi-Fi phone instead.

First, you're going to want to sign up for Skype with a $2.99 a month subscription for Unlimited Calls anywhere in the U.S. Then use your broadband wireless connection to connect to Skype wirelessly anywhere in your house (or anywhere with Wi-Fi) with a Wi-Fi phone such as the $150 Belkin Skype phone. Now you're saving $30-$50 a month on a home phone (or $300-$600 a year).

Just by lowering your mobile plan from the unlimited calling plan to the minimum calling plan (generally 400-500 minutes), you'll save about $50 a month, or $600 a year.

Check your usage on your wireless bill to determine how many minutes you actually use (as well as text messages, data, etc.). There's probably an opportunity to cut down. In most cases, you do not need to pay for a business line when you're starting out. If you're like the 80% of entrepreneurs who start solo working out of their home, you just need a separate number and voicemail box for business.

With Google Voice, you can create a new local phone number for free and forward it to any number —for instance, your mobile number. This is really helpful when you need to be able to answer your business line on the go. You can create a customized greeting for your business line as well as a customized voicemail message.

So forget about paying $100 a month for a business line. Get one for free with Google Voice.

Total savings: $2,700-$3,600 a year, or $225-$300 a month

Check into your prescriptions

Oh, those pharmaceutical companies. They're brilliant. They've figured out a way to get both you and your doctor convinced that the $75 a month brand name is better for you than the $25 a month generic. Bull.

If you have monthly prescriptions, these can be a significant expense – especially when you start paying for them on your own. Tell your doctor you're starting your own business and you can't afford your prescriptions anymore. Ask, "Is there a cheaper option?" Voila! Like magic, your doctor will tell you about the Name Brand Savings Card!

That's right. The 2008 recession hit drug companies hard. With so many unemployed, their "regulars" dropped off their name brand prescriptions like flies, so the drug companies came up with another magic formula: Perfect Price Discrimination. When regular subscribers, er, patients try to switch to a cheaper option, doctors can give them a savings card – many times 12 months worth of name brand prescription at the generic price.

These savings cards aren't available unless you ask. Doctors only give these savings cards to patients who need them. You're going to need it.

Total savings: $600 a year, or $50 a month

Cancel any unused memberships and subscriptions

Do you belong to a gym that you never use? Still subscribing to memberships, online services and magazines you don't read? Cut, cut, cut!

Total savings: $600-$2,400 a year, $50-$200 a month

Saving on the home office

You may be surprised to learn during this monthly budgeting exercise that you're going to save money simply by quitting your job. Things like monthly parking in your downtown office garage and going out for lunch can be significant expenses.

Unless you have a retail location, partners and employees, or otherwise absolutely need an office, you're probably like most entrepreneurs and you'll be starting out at home. Office space can cost anywhere from $10-$30 square feet a year depending on how expensive your city's commercial space is and you'll need about 250 square feet per person. Do you really need to be spending $10,000 a year on office space if it's just you? Probably not.

If you're going to be moving into the home office, you have more savings awaiting you: namely, a home office write-off. At tax time, you'll be able to write off your new office furniture, the printer, your computer, and the actual square footage your office occupies in your home.

Save on software and hardware with student discounts

If you're going to be buying a new computer, software, and peripherals for your business, find a student! Microsoft, Adobe, Dell, HP, Apple, and many other software and hardware providers offer serious (we're talking 50%-75%) discounts to students.

If you have a college student in your family – or if you're taking classes yourself, **buy these items at the college bookstore or online** at the student discount portal for that provider.

Don't forget to buy a backup service or hardware. Remember, you're on your own now and you're not going to have an IT guy there to save you when you accidentally delete your hard drive. Western Digital makes top notch and affordable 1 and 2 TB (terabyte) backup systems.

Keep your receipts for these items – you will write them off at tax time!

Total savings: $500-$1,000

Get Health Insurance for $50-$100 a month

It's a terrible, awful myth that you need to be "employed" in order to get health insurance. For a 30-year-old healthy male, **good health insurance can be as cheap as $50 a month**, depending on the level of coverage. That's right. Depending on how healthy – and how cost-conscious – your current employer's plan is, you may actually save money when you switch to an individual plan.

Right now, you're probably in a group plan with everyone else in your office. If you're younger and healthier than most of your office, you may be better off on your own! Frank, the 60-year-old guy down the hall who smokes and has a bad back is actually increasing the cost of your group plan.

Check your Explanation of Benefits Year End Summary from your current health insurance provider to see how much you actually spend on health care each year. If you get regular check-ups and have no outstanding health issues (beyond the occasional cold, flu, sinus infection, etc.), you and your health insurance provider are probably spending between $2,000 and $4,000 a year on your health care.

Why do people get health insurance? Well, generally so that if something terrible happens, they can afford health care. Unless you see some pretty expensive specialists on a regular basis, you're going to want to cover your out-of-pocket, routine expenses on your own (think of that $150 visit to your doctor to get antibiotics for your sinus infection) and get a plan that will cover the emergencies.

So, for now, let's look at high-deductible plans – plans that don't start paying for you until after you've reached a certain threshold of spending (the *deductible*). With a $2,500 deductible, you're paying your doctor's visits, you prescriptions, etc., until you reach $2,500 in annual spending – then the insurance plan kicks in and starts paying the rest.

Scenario 1
You spend $1,000 on prescriptions and doctor visits over 12 months. Your out-of-pocket expenses are the $1,000 you spent plus the $50-$100 a month you paid your insurance provider to insure against an emergency, expensive specialists, etc. (your *premium*). So you only pay $1,000 out of pocket and your monthly $50-$100 premium.

Scenario 2
You spend $1,000 on prescriptions and doctor visits over 11 months. Then, in November, you take a fall off a ladder and sprain your ankle badly, leading to a trip to the emergency room ($2,000), two visits to a specialist ($800), and four weeks of physical therapy ($1,500). That takes us to a total of $5,300 for just that year.

Your out of pocket expenses are the $1,000 you spent in the first 11 months, plus the $50-$100 a month you paid your insurance provider, plus another $1,500 in bills for the emergency before you reach your $2,500 deductible (threshold of out-of-pocket spending). So you only pay $2,500 out of pocket and your monthly $50-$100 premium.

Get quotes on eHealthInsurance, a free quote and application service that has up-to-date information on almost every major provider and plan on the planet. Quotes are based on your age, zip code, gender, etc. eHealthInsurance does a great job explaining the complexities of different health plans, the premiums, deductibles, lifetime maximums, etc., in easy-to-understand language.

Apply early - at least 2-3 months before you resign from your job. While it only takes an hour or so to fill out the detailed health insurance application, it can take 30-90 days for your application to be approved or denied and for your coverage to start.

Apply directly to the provider. Consider applying to more than one provider. If you are denied coverage from one provider – or if they review your application and decide to add permanent or temporary riders (restrictions on what they will cover), you will want to know early enough to apply to a different provider. Let's say you sprained your ankle two years ago; they won't cover orthopedic claims to that ankle for the next two years. You'll want to look at other options.

Pre-existing conditions holding you back? Get a broker. Insurance brokers are pros at finding the best deals and getting past the red tape. If you're having trouble finding insurance coverage on your own, talk to a professional – they may be able to help.

Another great option is your local Chamber of Commerce. Most chambers have group health plans for small businesses – even solo entrepreneurs. Most will require that you become a member of the Chamber of Commerce, which can run anywhere from $100 to $1,000 per year. Considering that this may be your only shot at health coverage as an entrepreneur, it's well worth the investment. In addition to health coverage, memberships to these organizations also open doors to advertising, networking opportunities, classes, and other benefits.

"Froogle" Shopping

If you're purchasing new equipment like a laptop – or just looking for a great deal on some special gizmo, look no further than Google's product search – also known as Froogle.com. Google tracks the prices and shipping costs of almost every product being sold online – whether it's through Amazon, eBay, or thousands of other small retailers. The site allows you to sort by total price (Retail Price + Shipping & Handling) to help you find the best deal online.

You'll save hours of searching and a lot of money simply by checking here first.

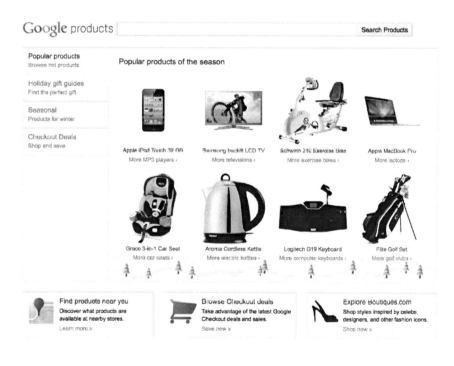

Use Coupon Codes Ruthlessly

As a **first-time customer**, there's usually a deal for you somewhere, but it may not be advertised. If you're buying in a store or hiring services, play the "starting a business" card and let them know that right now, "It's a little out of my price range... ." Most stores and service providers will be willing to cut you a break because they're making an investment in what they hope will be a long-time customer. Just make sure you live up to your end of the bargain: be a good customer.

At the start, you will be spending more on your business than ever, so use coupon and promo codes ruthlessly. If you are buying something online, generally in the checkout process there's a coupon or promotion code. Don't have one? Find one.

You can consistently knock **5%-30% off everything you buy online** just by searching "FedEx promo code" or "Office Depot coupon code" before you hit the checkout button. When you Google these terms, sites such as Retailmenot.com will pop up with current and expired codes. You may get free shipping, 15% off your first order, 20% off ink purchases – whatever. We're bootstrapping, here, people! We shall not pay retail!

Get 50% off on travel

Oh, the life of a traveling tumbleweed. If your startup requires a lot of travel, you need to tackle this expense pronto. Use sites like Priceline.com to get deals on hotel rooms and flights. Most of the time, you can get a hotel room at **50% off the normal rate**, just by creatively searching the hotels on Priceline by region and number of stars. If you search for a hotel in Cleveland and you know that there are only five four-star hotels on Priceline in the downtown area where you want to stay – and any of them will do – bid 50% the normal rate. You'll get it. From now on, you'll be staying in five-star hotels at the two-star price.

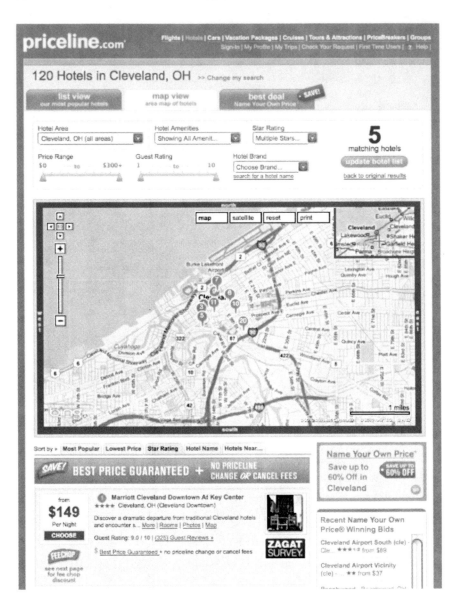

Another great way to save on lodging is by switching to a B&B instead of a hotel. They're more personal and generally nicer than the hotels and motels in the same price range. And breakfast is a LOT better. There are a surprising number of B&B's all over the country and you can generally book nice rooms with amenities for $75-$100 a night even in cities where the nicer hotels book at $200-

$250 a night.   Keep in mind, these folks don't have 24-hour desks, so a late arrival might not be an option.   If you're taking a late flight, call before you book – most B&B owners are flexible, but you don't want to find out that late check-in is a problem when you're locked out at 10 p.m.   Bed and Breakfast Online (www.bbonline.com) is a great resource.

3   Create a Business Model

"Ideas are like rabbits. You get a couple and learn how to handle them, and pretty soon you have a dozen."
— John Steinbeck

What is a Business Model?

A business model is the operational and financial blueprint of a company – the design of how value is marketed, purchased, and delivered. There are hundreds of different business models, from McDonald's, a franchise restaurant that sells fast food to consumers, to SAP, a company that sells software and professional services to large businesses, or to Zappos.com, an online shoe store.

Defining your Business Model

A business model can be defined by the answers to seven basic questions. By changing these elements, a business can develop new business models.

1. What is the need you fill or problem you solve? (Value Proposition)
2. Who are you selling to? (Target Market)
3. How will you reach your customers? (Sales/Marketing)
4. How do you produce your product or service? (Production)
5. How do you distribute your product or service? (Distribution)
6. How do you make money? (Revenue Model)
7. What are your costs? (Cost Structure)

Your business does not exist in a vacuum, so it's important to consider your market and your competition as you create your business model. We'll address these questions in more depth later on when we explore feasibility and branding.

8. How many competitors do you have? (Competition)
9. How will you differentiate your product or service? (Unique selling proposition)
10. How big is your market in dollars and is it growing or shrinking? (Market Size & Growth)
11. What percent of the market do you believe you could gain? (Market Share)

Types of Businesses

The following is by no means an exhaustive list of types of businesses, but will hopefully highlight several considerations when selecting a business model.

Lifestyle companies (for example, a "Four-Hour Workweek" business) are designed to create only as much profit as much as you need in order to have a comfortable lifestyle. Generally, these businesses have no employees, no physical location, and operate on an extremely variable basis.

Franchises (for example, McDonald's or Jiffy Lube) are proven business models that are pre-packaged (brand, operations, supply chain, etc.) and can be purchased. The entrepreneur works with the franchise organization to select a location, secure financing, get training, and launch their business and pay an upfront and ongoing fee to remain part of the franchise. These business models have inherently less risk because the business model has been proven and replicated by hundreds and thousands of business operators. The downside is that they have strict rules that must be followed in order to remain in compliance with the franchise.

Service businesses (for example, a landscaping company or an accounting firm) generally have lower startup costs than product companies, but are limited by manpower. Smaller startup costs means there's less to lose, but depending on the type of service and delivery model, these businesses may not be as scalable as product companies.

Product businesses include everything from food to electronics to clothing or manufacturing equipment. The design, manufacturing, packaging, and delivery of any product is a costly endeavor, so most product companies have relatively high startup costs, meaning more risk. The upside to product businesses is that if they take off, they're generally more scalable than services – meaning higher profits.

Bricks & mortar establishments such as retail stores and restaurants (franchise or non-franchise) require a keen understanding of the local market – including car traffic counts, neighborhood demographics, foot traffic, and other data. The upside is that the location and signage alone is a constant advertisement. The downside of these businesses is that they're limited to their location: If the neighborhood goes downhill, the business will be affected.

Spark Some Ideas on Springwise

Springwise.com is the world's leading sources of new business ideas, powered by a network of over 8,000 trend spotters. There are ideas in nearly every industry, including: automotive, the environment and sustainability, marketing and advertising, education, entertainment, financial services, fashion and beauty, food and beverage, gaming, government, homes and housing, lifestyle and leisure, media and publishing, and retail.

New business model trends are posted daily, so check out the archives to spark some ideas.

Components of a Business Model

Perhaps one of the most important books ever written about business models is "Business Model Generation," by Osterwalder, Pigneur, Smith, Van der Pijl, and Clark. The book can be purchased or downloaded at *ww.businessmodelgeneration.com.* The book is a must-read for understanding business-model components and how to visualize – or sketch out – a *new* business model.

If you're pursuing a classic, proven business model like a coffee shop or a dry cleaner, sketching out your business model may prove to be an exercise in the obvious, but it's still worth spending a few minutes mapping it out.

If you're contemplating a new business model – for example, transforming an in-person activity to an online activity – it's important to recognize that you'll face new risks. Plan to spend a lot of time sketching out your business model, from customers to value proposition to distribution channels to revenue streams and cost structures.

A new type of business model means heading into untested waters. You may find that customers prefer the in-person activity to the online activity – or it may be that your business model's revenue streams and cost structure don't line up the way you anticipate. These are the kinds of risks to be prepared for.

Customer Segments

Customers are the first (and most vital) component of a business model. Without customers, there is no revenue; without revenue, no business. Customer segments are distinct groups of customers that can be defined by demographics, psychographics, geography, behavior, or needs.

Customer segments are relevant to your business model in the sense that these distinct groups may interact very differently with your business. For instance, customer segments may require a distinct offer. Some may be looking more for features and functionality while others may be looking for price. This distinction will drive the kinds of marketing messages you send to each group: a glitzy brochure about the many functions of your Swiss Army Knife or a simple coupon for 50% off.

Customer segments may also interact through different distribution channels. Some may shop online; others may prefer to go to the store. They may also require different types of relationships. One type of Apple laptop buyer may never visit the store again, whereas another may sign up for every free class the store has to offer.

Because these customer segments can be so different in their preferences, need for support, etc, the profitability of each of these customer segments will also be different. The Apple buyer who signs up for every free in-store class costs the Apple store more, meaning the profit associated with that customer is less.

Make a list of all the potential types of users of your product, defined by the offer, channel, relationship, and profitability.

Value Proposition

Your value proposition is what makes your customer interested in your business – and ultimately why they need or want your product or service. The four basic types of value are functionality, reliability, convenience, and price, but other factors such as design, safety, brand or status, or even just newness can also be bases for value.

We'll explore your value proposition in more depth when we talk about your brand.

Revenue Streams

A revenue stream is simply how a business makes money. Revenue streams can be one-time or recurring transactions.
Some businesses have multiple revenue streams – for example, a software company that sells software and also sells training seminars.

The most basic type of revenue stream is the sale of a product or service. Other revenue streams include subscription fees, renting or leasing, licensing, brokerage fees, service contracts, insurance, events, and advertising revenue.

Make a list of all your potential revenue streams – product sales, service contracts, subscriptions, etc. – and mark whether they are one-time or potentially recurring revenue streams and how much you could make in a single transaction.

Channels

Your channels are your connections with your customer – how you communicate with them, how you sell to them, and how you deliver your product or service to them. Channels can take the form of sales people, websites, retail stores, or wholesale distributors. Channels help raise awareness for your product or service, help customers evaluate the product or service, and allow them to make a purchase. In some cases, channels may also offer post-sales support like product returns or service.

A Ford dealership is a channel for the Ford Motor Company. There, customers can test drive, evaluate, and purchase a car. Later, they can also go to their dealership for service on their car.

Make a list of all your potential channels of distribution and marketing. How can you get your product out to more stores? How can you get your brand in front of more customers?

Customer Relationships

There are many types of customer relationships, and they vary in intensity and cost. Self-service and automated service customer relationships are low-intensity and require very limited interaction. An example of a self-service or automated service relationship is an automatic car wash.

Other types of relationships require more interaction, such as personal assistance. Bank tellers offer personal assistance, whereas ATMs offer self-service. Personal assistance helps form real relationships with people that are stickier than non-personal relationships. The downside is that personal assistance generally costs more to deliver. In some cases, the cost can be passed on to the customer, like the cost of a pizza delivery boy or the cost of a broker. In most cases, however, it's an additional expense for the business.

Communities where customers interact with each other and with the business are another type of relationship. Software User Groups (for example, accountants who use SAP) are one such example.

Key Resources

Key resources refer to the building blocks of your product or service. If you're going to sell handmade knit slippers, you're going to need a lot of yarn. In this case, the yarn is a raw material for your product, and therefore a key resource to your business. Key resources could be materials, the people you employ to sell your product, or the website you need to market your product online.

Make a list of these key resources. What are you going to need in order to market, produce, and sell your product or service?

Key Activities

Key activities for a product company could include things like marketing, taking orders, production, packaging, shipping, billing, and customer feedback

Map out all of the key activities you need to do in order to market, produce, distribute, and get paid.

Key Partnerships

Your business will likely rely on other businesses and individuals outside your organization in order to be successful. Strategic partnerships, endorsements, R&D, manufacturing, and wholesale distribution are just a few examples of types of key partnerships.

Write down all the key partnerships that could help make your business successful.

Cost Structure

Your cost structure is the most important component to your profitability next to revenue streams. Businesses encounter two types of costs: fixed costs and variable costs.

Fixed costs are those that the business incurs regardless of sales – things like rent, utilities, and furniture. Variable costs can be adjusted and right-sized depending on the needs of the business at the moment – for instance, raw materials or advertising.

A business has economies of scale when it can easily ramp up production and serve more customers without investing much more in fixed costs. Scalability – or economies of scale – is extremely desirable for sustainable and profitable growth.

Make a list of all of your costs, fixed and variable. How scalable is your business model? If you made your business a hundred times bigger, would it be more profitable per unit, less profitable per unit, or about the same?

Sketch Out Your Business Model

Whether you are selling a product in a retail store or selling a service online, you need a clear visual picture of your business model. This includes your customer, value proposition, channel, customer relationship, revenue stream, and costs.

Step 1: Create two simple sentences

What do you sell? To whom? We sell _____ to _____.
How do you make money? This is how we get paid …

Example: a Used College Textbook Website
We sell discounted, used textbooks to college students online. We get paid 5% of the book price ($100 book = $5 for us).

Step 2: Make it Visual – and Fill in all the Details

Materials needed:
Whiteboard or large paper
Post-it Notes

Process:
Fill in process points
This is how the customer finds us
. This is how they make a purchase
This is how the service/product order is fulfilled
. Other steps
Attach costs to each process point
Advertising
. Transaction
Packaging
. Shipping
Customer support people

Classic Business Model Strategies

What's your strategy? How are you going to dominate your market? Jim Muehlhausen, an expert on business model strategy at the Business Model Institute explains several classic business model strategies as well as a way to evaluate new business models at *www.businessmodelinstitute.com*. Here are just a few popular strategies.

Disruption
eBay, Craig's List

Taking an outdated process like listing classified ads and disrupting it with low-cost technology (like Craig's List) is one of the most powerful business models. This is exactly what Google did to the Yellow Pages and what the mini steel mills did to the steel industry. These business models take whole industries and turn them upside down – changing them forever and capitalizing on the new opportunities.

Harvard Business School's Clayton Christensen is the foremost expert on disruptive business models and has written several books on the topic, including The Innovator's Solution.

The Health Club Model (Subscription)

Two defining components of a subscription-based business model are:

1. An automated recurring revenue (like an automatically deducted monthly payment plan)
2. Use-it-or-lose-it pricing (whether you workout or not, you pay). This shifts the risk of usage to the customer.

Examples of this model are country clubs, cable television, and timeshares.   Service contracts, warranties, and many Internet subscription sites are also good examples of this business model.

Network Effect
Facebook, LinkedIn

Network effect happens when users derive value not only through their own use of a product, but through others' use of the product as well. A telephone is an example of a technology that requires a network in order to be beneficial; someone has to be on the other end with a telephone in order for it to work.

Networks can create natural monopolies through "lock-in," the effect whereby users are wedded to the network because switching to another network is either too costly or too inconvenient. For instance, switching from MySpace to Facebook would involve getting your friends to switch as well.

A network effect can exist in combination with other strategies. For instance, Etsy and CrowdSpring, with their communities of thousands of individual designers, both enjoy network effect and also serve the Long Tail. Multi-site retail locations can also have network effect when multiple locations make service delivery meaningfully more convenient.

Niche & Long Tail Models

The Internet has made it possible to instantly enter a worldwide market with almost any product or service. With a nearly unlimited geographic reach, businesses can cater to ever-smaller niches.

An example of this niche model is an online store that sells nothing but handmade Norwegian Christmas tree ornaments.

Amazon, iTunes, eBay, and Etsy are all excellent examples of platforms that enable the Long Tail. Revenue models are diverse in the Long Tail and go far beyond niche product sales to include merchant, direct manufacturer, ad-supported, subscription, affiliate, licensing, brokerage, infomediary, and community revenue models.

Two well-known authorities on Long Tail and niche business models are Chris Anderson, author of "The Long Tail" and Timothy Ferriss, author of "The Four Hour Work Week."

Serve the Gold Miners in the Gold Rush

The gold rush of 1849 brought thousands of aspiring gold miners to California. However, for every miner that struck it rich, thousands failed. A more profitable and sustainable business model than mining gold was selling supplies and services to miners. Companies such as Wells Fargo and Levi Strauss were born as service companies to gold miners.

A recent example of this was the real estate speculation of the mid 2000's — where mortgage brokers and homebuilders capitalized on the gold-rush mentality of homebuyers — and made out far better than the homebuyers themselves.

Trump Model
Starbucks, Haagen Daz, Panera Bread, Coach handbags

Until the recent recession, consumers seemed ever willing to buy upscale everything. Why brew coffee at home when you can buy a $4.00 venti mochachino from Starbucks?

This business model aims to define to the top end of the market and is typically high-profit. Donald Trump has made his entire fortune from this business model.

Low-Cost Provider
Wal-Mart, UPS, Southwest Airlines

If you are a low-cost provider, your customers are bargain hunters. Access to low-cost vendors, vertical integration, and controlling the distribution channel are just a few ways to become a low-cost provider. Low cost can be obtained through operational excellence like Wal-Mart or UPS or through a limited offering such as Southwest Airline's use of only 737 aircraft.

Done correctly, this tactic can be the most powerful business model strategy. However, simply selling for less will lower your margin and destroy your profits. For the low-cost provider model to be sustainable, you have to maintain your margin.

Your business model will change

Your business model will evolve over time as you adapt in response to opportunities and threats. Review your business model frequently – in the beginning, quarterly. Look for ways to improve your margin and operations and pay close attention to new business model strategies that emerge in your industry and other industries.

20 Factors for Evaluating a Business Model

		Worst	Best
1	**Market Need**	Nice to have	Necessary to live
2	**Unique Selling Proposition**	Commodity	Unique
3	**Competitors**	Many	None
4	**Market Size**	Small	Large
5	**Market Growth**	Shrinking	Growing
6	**Longevity**	Fad	Timeless
7	**Price**	Highest priced offering	Lowest priced offering
8	**Margin**	Lowest margin in industry	Highest margin in industry
9	**Follow-on Revenue Opportunities**	One-time sale, no upselling opportunity	Recurring sales, lots of upselling opportunities
10	**Target Market**	Undefined, unknown	Well-defined, segmented, known
11	**Customers**	Cheap, not loyal	Rich, loyal
12	**Sales**	Hard to sell, costly to sell	No effort required
13	**Advertising**	Hard to quantify return on advertising	Directly quantifiable advertising results
14	**Startup Costs**	Large	Small
15	**Barriers to Entry**	Insurmountable	None
16	**Scalability**	Not scalable	Scalable
17	**Predictability**	Unpredictable, subject to regulation and other outside forces	Predictable, not subject to outside forces
18	**Intellectual Property**	Impossible to patent, trademark, or protect	Patentable, protectable
19	**Exit**	No clear buyers, low multiples	Many buyers, high multiples
20	**Return on Investment**	Negative	High, guaranteed

4   Feasibility

"The general who wins the battle makes many calculations in his temple before the battle is fought. The general who loses makes but few calculations beforehand."
— *Sun Tzu*

In this chapter, we're going to do some very simple math that will save you the pain and agony of launching a business that's set up to fail. It's a far better strategy to abandon a bad idea at infancy and go back to the drawing board than to try to force an unrealistic outcome.

Opportunity-focused entrepreneurs start with the customer and the market in mind. They analyze the market to determine industry issues, market size and structure, growth, barriers to entry, and potential market share.

But **big markets aren't enough**. We'll also examine your cost structure, the core economics of your business, and the time to breakeven.

This section is organized in a step-wise fashion, with nine steps split up into three groups: profitability, market potential, and actual demand for your offering. There are nine tests in total and each should take you a few minutes to complete as long as you have the information handy. If at any point your business fails one of the tests, consider putting a bullet in this particular project and moving on.

The purpose of this section is to evaluate your business idea to see if it's worth pursuing. Your business model must pass **three tests for profitability**:

1. **Unit Profitability**
2. **Operational Profitability**
3. **Investment Profitability**

First we're going to estimate the basic financial feasibility of your business by examining your unit costs and revenue to determine whether your business will be profitable at the unit level. This is unit profitability.

Then we'll look at the overhead costs of your business to determine whether your model is sustainable and can support you with a salary and pay the rent. This is operational profitability.

Then we'll examine the startup costs and time to breakeven to determine whether your business is a good investment for you and for others. This is investment profitability.

Next, we'll look at the feasibility of your business in the context of the marketplace, examining the market from the top down and from the bottom up. Your business will need to pass **three tests for market attractiveness**:

1. **Top-down** Market Share (%) of Market Size
2. **Bottoms-up** List of Target Customers & Revenue
3. **Performance of Similar Businesses**

Here, we'll quantify potential demand with data. Once we've determined the overall market size and market opportunity, we'll look at how similar businesses are performing in your industry and market.

Finally, we'll check our work by talking to some potential customers to determine if there's real demand for your specific offering. It's impossible to determine whether people will make a purchase until they actually pull out their checkbooks, but we're going to simulate demand on a micro-level with individual potential customers to determine interest, demand and price point. Your business will need to pass three tests for demand and price sensitivity:

1. **Indication of interest** from potential customers through personal interviews, surveys, field trials, or observation
2. **Factors driving demand**
3. **Willingness to pay:** price point

By the end of these exercises you will be able to make an informed choice as to whether your idea is still practical and attractive.

Feasibility Project Plan

Before you spend another hour – or a single dime – on your idea, let's make sure the math works!

Profitability
1. Unit Economics: Unit Price – Unit Costs = Unit Profit
2. Monthly Burn Rate / Unit Profit = Minimum Units
3. Startup Costs, Time to Break Even, Sensitivity Tables

Market Attractiveness
4. Top Down – Market Sizes & Growth, Market Share % of Total Market
5. Bottoms up – Target Customer List, Target $, Probability
6. Performance of a Similar Business (Foot Traffic or Internet Traffic)

Actual Demand for Your Offering
7. Indication of Interest – Interviews, Surveys, Field Trials, and Observation of Potential Customers
8. Factors Driving Demand
9. Willingness to Pay

Are you ready? Because in this 24-hour sprint of research and calculations, we're going to determine whether you should proceed with your idea – or go back to the drawing board.

Test 1: Unit Profitability (Unit Economics)

Unit economics are the smallest building block – the atomic level – of your business. If the unit economics of your business are negative, no amount of scale or pizzazz is going to make it profitable. This is the *most important equation* in this book. Unit economics are simply the

Unit Retail Price – Unit Costs = Profit per Unit

Unit economics - or profit per unit – are usually much better at scale than at startup. At startup, businesses typically have difficult payment terms – for instance, a supplier may require a deposit since you're a new customer or a manufacturer may charge more for smaller quantities or have a large minimum order size.

Make a list of all your unit costs before scale and at scale. We're more concerned with the numbers that are "at scale", but keep in mind that if your business doesn't succeed, you may never get to scale.

There are three types of costs:
1. **One-time startup costs** are capital expenses like furniture, computers, fixtures, and equipment.
2. **Monthly recurring overhead costs** are fixed monthly costs such as salaries, benefits, rent, utilities, loan payments, insurance, internet, and phone.
3. **Unit costs** are costs that can be specifically associated with each unit. For instance, at McDonald's, unit costs would include cups, straws, hamburger buns, ketchup, and beef patties.

List all your unit costs. Once you have all your unit costs listed, double check to make sure that you haven't forgotten anything – even if it's a small number. Some businesses have margins that are less than 10%, so even a 2-3% credit card transaction fee is significant.

For a product company, the minimum orders and manufacturing setup fees can make the before-scale and at-scale unit profits very different. The chart below shows just a few typical unit costs for a product company.

Example Product Company

Before Scale	At Scale
Setup fee	
Minimum order size	*Optimal order size*
Cost per unit	Cost per unit
Advertising	Advertising
Shipping	Shipping
Packaging	Packaging
Wholesale distributor %	Wholesale distributor %
Transaction costs	Transaction costs
Sales Tax	Sales Tax

The unit cost of a service company is the cost to serve one customer once. The major unit cost for most service companies is labor – the hourly rate of an employee. Service companies are generally speaking less scalable than product companies, so the unit cost is pretty much the same before scale and at scale. The major difference is labor utilization; before your business takes off, you may be paying people to sit around (working on revenue-producing jobs 50% of the time instead of 100% of the time).

Example Service Company

Before Scale	At Scale
Advertising	Advertising
Materials	Materials
Labor	*Labor*
Transaction costs	Transaction costs
Sales Tax	Sales Tax

Test 2: Operational Profitability (Monthly Burn Rate)

Now that you have a firm handle on your personal finances, figure out how much *you* need to live. What is your *personal* monthly burn rate?

Let's say you that you need $4,000 a month to live (food, housing, car, etc.). How many widgets do you have to sell each month in order to survive?

Next, let's add your salary and the other monthly recurring overhead costs of your business (such as rent, utilities, Internet, phone, servers) to determine the total monthly burn rate of the business. These expenses are overhead expenses – and these bills come every month whether your making sales or not.

Now, from the unit economics calculations, find the profit per unit and divide the monthly burn rate by the profit per unit.

Monthly Burn Rate / Profit Per Unit = Units Per Month

The result is the number of units you have to sell every month in order to survive. Now, in order to be profitable (have money left over after overhead and unit costs), you'll have to sell even more.

Answer the following questions:
1. How many units do you need to sell in a month in order to live?
2. How many units do you need to sell in a year?
3. Is this reasonable?

If your business does not pass this test, stop! It's time to re-evaluate.

Test 3: Investment Profitability (Startup Costs)

We're finished with the major portion of our feasibility analysis. If you've survived the first two calculations, your business model is in pretty good shape.

Now let's take a look at your startup costs. If you're launching a new software, how much is it going to cost to build? If you're launching a new product, how much are the manufacturing setup costs (tools, dies, etc.)? If you're opening up the store, how much will the build out cost you?

Startup costs are unique to every business, but here are a few estimates just to get you started:

Legal incorporation and documentation – $250
Website (simple) – $2,000-5,000
Logo and business cards – $2,000
Computer and software – $3,000

List out your startup costs and get rough estimates, actual bids, or prices for each item. Add all the one-time startup costs together to get your total cost to start up.

Time to Breakeven

A business "breaks even" when it sells enough product to repay all of its startup costs. To determine how many widgets you need to sell in order to repay your startup costs, divide your startup costs by your profit per unit. To determine how long it will take to break even, use the following equation:

Months to Breakeven =

Startup Costs
((Profit per Unit x Monthly Units Sold) – Monthly Burn)

How long should it take to break even?

Time to breakeven varies widely from industry to industry. Service businesses generally have lower startup costs and therefore break even faster. Higher startup costs means that it takes longer to break even.

The more profitable a company is at the unit and operational level, the faster it pays back its startup costs and breaks even.

If you can pay your startup costs back in a year or two, you're in good shape. If it's going to take longer than a few years, take a hard look at whether this business is a good investment of your time and money. A lot can go wrong in three years. A longer time to breakeven means a higher the risk of investment – and a lower the return on investment (ROI).

For service companies, one to two years to breakeven is ideal and for product companies, one to three years to breakeven is ideal.

What if the math doesn't work?

Make sure that the potential revenue of your business far outweighs your startup costs. If you need $1 million to get started, but your business model only makes $10,000 a year, that's a problem. Venture capital and angel investors aren't interested in investing in a company that makes just enough to cover personal living expenses, and traditional banks are not interested in lending to a business that can't afford to pay back its loans.

If the math doesn't work now – before you've even started – then stop! Go back to the drawing board. As human beings we have a tendency to fall in love with our ideas. Make sure that you fall in love with a profitable idea.

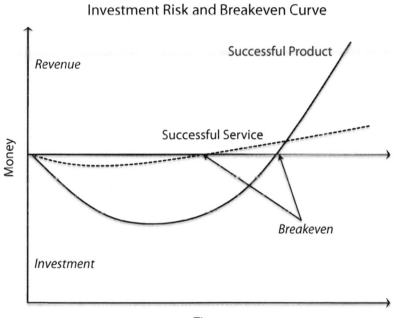

Investment Risk and Breakeven Curve

		One-Time Start-Up Costs	
	1	Purchase price or downpayment if buying a business	$0.00
	2	Office furniture	$2,000.00
	3	Computer hardware and software	$2,500.00
	4	Setup, installation and consulting fees	$0.00
	5	Business cards and stationery (design & printing)	$700.00
	6	Decorating and remodeling	$0.00
	7	Fixtures, counters, equipment & Installation	$0.00
	8	Starting inventory, raw materials, tools, etc.	$0.00
	9	Deposits with public utilities	$0.00
	10	Legal and other professional fees	$500.00
	11	Business licenses and permits	$0.00
	12	Advertising and promotion for opening	$2,000.00
	13	Signage	$0.00
	14	Rent & security deposit (often equals 3 months rent)	$0.00
	15	Operating Cash	$0.00
	16	Website	$5,000.00
	17	Other	$0.00
	18	Other	$0.00
	19	Other	$0.00
	20	Other	$0.00
		Subtotal	$12,700.00
		Monthly Expenses	
	17	Salary of owner-manager (amount you need to pay yourself)	$5,000.00
	18	All other salaries, wages, & commissions	$0.00
	19	Payroll taxes or self-employment tax	$0.00
	20	Rent	$0.00
	21	Equipment lease payments	$0.00
	22	Advertising (print, broadcast and Internet)	$300.00
	23	Postage & shipping costs	$0.00
	24	Supplies (inks, toners, labels, paper goods, etc.)	$100.00
	25	Telephone	$200.00
	26	Utilities	$0.00
	27	Internet connection	$50.00
	28	Website hosting and maintenance	$20.00
	29	General business insurance	$0.00
	30	Business vehicle insurance	$0.00
	31	Health insurance	$100.00
	32	Interest & principal on loans & credit cards	$0.00
	33	Inventory, raw materials, parts	$0.00
	34	Legal and other professional fees	$0.00
	35	Franchise fee	$0.00
	36	Other	$0.00
	37	Other	$0.00
	38	Other	$0.00
	39	Other	$0.00
		Subtotal	$5,770.00
		Calculate total start-up funds	
	40	Estimate the number of months needed to find customers and get established	4
	41	**Monthly expense for months**	$23,080.00
	42	**One time start-up expense**	$12,700.00
	43	**Total start-up costs**	**$35,780.00**

Market-driven feasibility

While big markets alone won't make your business successful, small markets will definitely limit your opportunities. There are three ways to calculate market attractiveness and whether a market is big enough to support you and your competitors:

1. Top Down – Market Share % of Total Market
2. Bottoms up – Target Customers
3. Sales of Similar Businesses

Test 1: Top-down Market Size

Industries and trade groups often have statistics on the size of their industry, growth, major players, and trends. Use these data sources to estimate your potential sales. If you have trouble finding good data sources, call the industry trade group directly – they may be able to point you in the right direction or they may know the answers to your market size questions off the top of their heads.

If your customers are publicly traded companies, you're in luck. There's a wealth of free information available about their operations, strategies, and financial performance available in their annual reports. Market research firms and other industry analysts also publish reports on specific companies and industries that can be purchased and downloaded for around $100, but can range in price from $10-$10,000.

Sometimes, especially in the case of new business models, the industry and market data that's available isn't entirely what you need to determine your potential market size, so you'll have to do a bit of your own calculations. For example, when the founders of Netflix wanted to figure out what their potential market size might be, no one was yet sending DVDs in the mail, so there wasn't much useful data about the DVD-by-mail market. Instead, they had to use data about companies like Blockbuster and other video rental stores in order to estimate the potential market size and find data on video rental sales.

Resource & Website	Description
US Census Bureau www.census.gov	Search for industry information by SIC or NAICS classification or search for demographic and population info by geography
Hoovers www.hoovers.com	Find competitors, revenues, and executive summaries of public and private companies
EDGAR Online www.sec.gov/edgar.shtml	Annual Reports (10k Filings) and other financial reports on publicly traded companies
Dun & Bradstreet www.dnb.com	Company and industry information
ThomasNet www.thomasnet.com	Supplier and manufacturer information
CrunchBase www.crunchbase.com	Database of technology companies, key people, and investors
Compete www.compete.com	Internet traffic, referring sites
Alexa www.alexa.com	Internet traffic, audience demographics
Spyfu www.spyfu.com	Competitor's Internet keywords and ad words

Hoovers provides detailed information about industries and companies, both public and private. The site provides much of this information for free, allowing you to browse major players, total industry sales, and other data easily.

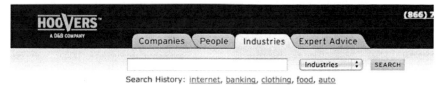

Search History: internet, banking, clothing, food, auto

Hoover's Directories > Industry Overviews > Internet Search & Navigation Services

Internet Search & Navigation Services

Overview

Industry Description

Companies that own and operate search engines and other categorized Web sites used to find information on the Internet.

SIC: 8999 | **NAICS:** 51811, 518112, 519130

Related Industries:

Development Tools, Operating Systems & Utilities Software, Information Collection & Delivery, Internet Content Providers, Internet & Online Services Providers

To get access to the full industry record, register now.

Top 5 Companies

Company	Sales	Location
Google Inc.	23,650.56M	Mountain View, CA
Yahoo! Inc.	6,460.31M	Sunnyvale, CA
Yahoo Japan Corporation	3,019.09M	Tokyo, Japan
NHN Corporation	954.42M	Seongnam, Gyeonggi
Baidu, Inc.	650.71M	Beijing, China

There are 42 companies in this industry. To view all of them, register now.

Once you have a good idea of the Total Addressable Market (TAM), estimate your market share by dividing the market size by the number of players. For instance, if the market size is $100 million and there are 100 companies in the industry, the "average" revenue per company is about $1 million. The U.S. Census Bureau has data organized by industry (NAICS or SIC code), including the total industry sales and number of firms per industry.

Averages can be deceiving, so check to see how the industry is organized – are there just a few players who control most of the market? Estimate your initial market share as equal to that of your smallest competitor, or estimate your share as equaling the average competitor in the market.

Test 2: Bottoms-up Target Customer List

Market sizes help define the ceiling of your sales potential – a limit to what is possible. Now we need to explore what's realistic. It's unusual to be the only player in a market, so how much can you actually sell?

One way to estimate your actual sales is by building a target customer list. If you're marketing to businesses, the list is pretty straightforward. Which businesses do you think are actual potential customers? How much could you sell to each? What's the probability of a sale?

Target Customer	Target Revenue	Probability
Bath & Body Works	$100,000	20%
The Body Shop	$500,000	30%
Sephora	$400,000	20%

If your customers are consumers, try to be as specific as possible. For instance, if you're marketing to vegetarians in the U.S., how many vegetarians are there? Well, according to some quick research, there are 7.3 million vegetarians in the US. Who are they?

A survey of 5,050 adults conducted by Harris Interactive Service Bureau and Vegetarian Times shows that "3.2 percent of U.S. adults, or 7.3 million people, follow a vegetarian-based diet. In addition, 10 percent of U.S. adults, or 22.8 million people, say they largely follow a vegetarian-inclined diet. 59 percent are female; 41 percent are male. 42 percent are age 18 to 34 years old; 40.7 percent are 35 to 54; and 17.4 percent are over 55." This is the type of information that you'll need to find in order to convince yourself –

and lenders and investors – that your market is big enough for your business.

If you are marketing to a group based on demographics or geography – for instance "single mothers in Iowa City" – start with the Census data. The U.S. Census Bureau has household and population demographic information such as age, gender, income, and education readily available for free at www.census.gov.

Test 3: Sales of a Similar Business

One of the most reliable ways to estimate the revenue potential of a new business is to look at similar businesses. For instance, if you're opening a coffee shop, check out coffee shops in the neighborhood next door. How are they performing?

Below is a screenshot of CrunchBase, a database of technology companies that shows information like web traffic and number of users. In most cases, web traffic data is available from the time the site went live. Check out your competitors – how long did it take them to get traction? What was their growth trajectory like? This is an important piece of data for creating reasonable market share growth trajectories.

If your competitors use the web to market or sell their product or service, make sure to check into their web traffic. What are the demographics of their audience? Where do they get most of their traffic?

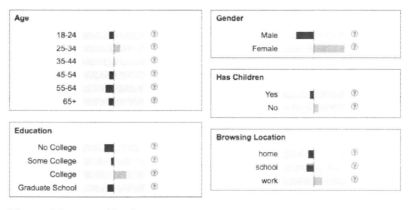

Advanced Demographics for zappos.com

Audience breakdown by income, ethnicity, age, education, gender, children and browsing location.

Get Clarity with Sensitivity Tables

A sensitivity table shows a range of potential outcomes given two variables. In this case, we want to get more clarity on the profit potential of your company, so we're going to look at Profit Margin (profit per unit) and the Number of Units Sold.

List your potential Margin (Profit Per Unit) low to high (as below) and the number of units (or customers) you could potentially sell in one year. Then, in each cell, multiply the number at the top of the column with the number at the front of the row. The results can be eye opening.

Sensitivity tables are extremely valuable in revealing the true risk and the true potential of business models, so spend a good amount of time with this exercise and investigate all the potential scenarios and outcomes for your business.

	Number Sold		
Margin	**1,000**	**10,000**	**100,000**
$5.00	$5,000	$5,000	$5,000
$7.50	$7,500	$75,000	$750,000
$10.00	$10,000	$100,000	$1,000,000

Feasibility Project Plan

Profitability

1. Unit Economics: Unit Price – Unit Costs = Unit Profit

   Unit Profit = $_____ per unit

2. Monthly Burn Rate / Unit Profit = Minimum Units

   Minimum Units = _____ per month

3. Startup Costs = $_____

   Time to Breakeven = _____ months

Sensitivity Table:

Profit per Unit	Units Sold		
	Low_____	Med_____	High_____
Low_____			
Med_____			
High_____			

Market Attractiveness

4. Top Down – Market Size _____, % growth _____%

   Market Share % of Total Market _____%

5. Bottoms up – Target Customers, Revenue, Probability

Target Customer	Target Revenue	Probability
	$_____	___%
	$_____	___%
	$_____	___%

6. Similar Business Sales $_____

Actual Demand for your offering

7. Interest: Is there demand? Will anyone buy this?
8. Decision: What factors are driving their decision?
9. Willingness to Pay: Average Price Point $_____

Actual Demand For Your Offering

1. Indication of interest
2. Factors driving their decision
3. Willingness to Pay: Pricing your offer

If you've made it this far in the feasibility tests, you're doing really well. Your business model is profitable and there's a large enough market to support it. The question now is this: Will anyone buy? And just as importantly, how much are they willing to pay?

Indication of Interest: Probably the easiest way to find out is just to ask them – and we'll do that with surveys or personal interviews. But most people find it hard to just come out and say "No, I don't like your idea." So we're going to trick them into giving us straight answers.

Selecting your offer: The trick comes in the disguise. We're going to disguise your offering inside three offerings and ask people to pick their favorite. One offer will be your actual concept; the other two will be decoys. It sounds like a circus trick, but this is how we buy things every day – whether it's online, in a retail store, or in a corporate boardroom.

Willingness to Pay: Finally, we need to figure out what to charge. So, we're going to ask potential customers and Average Joe. How much will your customer pay for your offering? There are three ways to ask this question. Interestingly enough, you'll get different answers, so ask the question all three ways.

1. How much would you pay?
2. If you were in my shoes, how much would you charge?
3. Guess how much this offering costs? (The Price is Right)

Uncovering Demand: the Market Research Process

1. Select your research method
2. Build your list of questions
3. Create your list of market research participants

If possible, choose more than one type of research method – like personal interviews for qualitative information and an online survey for quantitative information.

Build your initial list of questions with your business model in mind: specifically, price and quantity. Your list of questions will evolve as you get more and more insight about your target customer. **Here's what we're trying to find out** with this research:

- Is this idea feasible in the marketplace? Do your customers know something that you don't know? Why doesn't this product or service already exist?
- Is there demand? Do people actually want to buy this product or service?
- How much are they willing to pay?
- Will they buy more than once?
- What factors are driving their decision?
- What objections will customers have to buying your product or service?

Market research participants should be part of your target market. If you're marketing to single moms, talk to single moms that you know as well as single moms that you don't know. The more participants and information, the better.

1. Ask them directly: "Would you buy?" and "How much would you pay?"
2. Compare three offers: "Which one(s) would you buy?" and "Guess the price."
3. Field test your offering (on the shelf, online, etc.)

Indication of interest: Direct Market Research

While there are many ways to perform market research, most
businesses use one of five basic methods:
1. Surveys
2. Focus groups
3. Personal interviews
4. Observation
5. Field trials

The method of research you choose depends on how much money
you're willing to spend and which method will give you the
information you need. Surveys, personal interviews, and
observation are three types of research that are fairly inexpensive
because you can do them yourself. Focus groups and field trials are
a little more expensive because they require trained professionals or
specialized market research environments.

Qualitative and Quantitative Information

Surveys are best for quantitative information: *"What percentage* of
people own dogs?"* Personal interviews and focus groups are best
for qualitative information: *"Why* do you prefer dogs?"

Quantitative questions typically start off with when, where, what
percentage or how many. Qualitative questions dig into the why.
Whether you combine different types of market research – for
instance, a survey and a few personal interviews – make sure that
when you build your list of questions, you're getting both the
quantitative information you need as well as the qualitative
information that will give you insight.

Surveys

With concise and straightforward questionnaires, you can analyze a sample group that represents your target market. The larger the sample size (number of participants), the more reliable your survey results will be.

In-person surveys are one-on-one interviews typically conducted in high-traffic locations such as shopping malls or office buildings. They allow you to present people with samples of products, packaging, or advertising and gather immediate feedback. In-person surveys are great because you can reach a large audience of strangers and have an interactive conversation with them. In-person surveys can generate response rates of more than 90%.

SurveyMonkey.com
because knowledge is everything

Online surveys are fast, simple and inexpensive – in most cases, free. Online surveys are a great tool for collecting objective and subjective information about customer opinions and preferences. The downside of online surveys is that they don't work if your target customer is not online. Children, older adults, and rural demographics can be tough to reach online, so this is not the best format for them.

Telephone surveys are another option for an interactive, conversational survey, but convincing people to participate can be tough. When you're calling complete strangers with a telephone survey, you may only see a response rate of 50% to 60% at best.

Mail surveys are a relatively inexpensive way to reach a broad audience, but they only generate response rates of 3% to 15%.

How to create an online survey

1. Establish the goals of your survey. What you want to learn?
2. Determine your sample. Who you will interview?
3. Create your questionnaire. What will you ask? Keep the questions short and sweet. The survey should be under 10 questions, on one page, and take only a few minutes to complete.
4. Pre-test and proofread the questionnaire before you send it out.
5. Send the survey out to a small test group first and make sure that the questions are understood clearly.
6. Send the survey out your full list of participants, collect your responses, and analyze your results.

SurveyMonkey allows you to create 15 different types of custom questions with scales, check boxes, essay boxes, multiple choice, and more. Once you've created your survey, you can collect responses over e-mail, Facebook, or even embed the survey on your website.

Send a sample to a small subset of people (10-15) initially to test out your survey and make sure that all the questions make sense   and that you're getting the information you need. It's better to find out if you need to make changes before you've sent the survey out to hundreds of people.

Where do you live?
- ○ North Western United States
- ○ South Western United States
- ○ Mid Western United States
- ○ New England United States
- ○ Southern United States
- ○ South Eastern United States
- ○ Other [   ]

Would you use an online trading system?
- ○ Yes
- ○ No
- ○ Not sure

What's the range of your portfolio size (US dollars)?
- ○ Less than $1K
- ○ Between $2-5K
- ○ Between $6-20K
- ○ Between $21-100K
- ○ Between $101-999K
- ○ More than $1M

What would you pay for an online trading system (US dollars)?
- ○ Would not use one
- ○ Less than $20/month
- ○ Between $21-30/month
- ○ Between $31-60/month
- ○ Between $61-100/month
- ○ More than $100/month

What's your education level?
- ○ Completed high school
- ○ Completed college
- ○ Completed graduate school
- ○ PHD

Personal interviews

Personal interviews are conversations that are more in-depth and interactive than surveys. They generally include unstructured, open-ended questions and last for about an hour.

Personal interviews and focus groups provide more subjective data than surveys. The results are not statistically reliable, which means that they don't represent a large enough segment of the population. Nevertheless, interviews yield valuable insights into customer attitudes and are excellent ways to uncover issues related to new products and services.

The downside of personal interviews is that they may come with some bias. If you know the person that you're interviewing, make sure they're not just telling you what you want to hear. Ask them what they don't like about the offering – or what the risks are in your business model. Make sure that they know that the purpose of your interview is to uncover the truth of whether this opportunity is worth pursuing.

Don't count on promises. Many people ask potential customers, "Would you buy this product?" The problem with this question is that it's much easier for consumers to say "yes" to a hypothetical question than it is to actually change their behavior and buy a new product or service from a new business.

Focus groups

In professionally facilitated focus groups, a moderator uses a scripted series of questions or topics to lead a discussion among a group of people. These sessions take place at neutral locations, usually at facilities with videotaping equipment and an observation room with one-way mirrors. A focus group usually lasts one to two hours. It takes at least three groups to get balanced results. These specialized focus group centers don't come cheap – costing between $5,000 and $20,000 per session.

If you can't afford the expense, but feel that a group discussion will help you get the answers you need, try creating your own focus group. Find a quiet, neutral location like a school classroom or a library conference room and recruit one to three groups of four to six target respondents to participate.

Create a detailed list of questions for your group. Open the conversation by giving the group some background about the business concept. Guide the discussion around your main questions, but don't dominate the conversation.

If possible, have a friend facilitate the conversation for you and report back. People many times feel uncomfortable giving negative feedback, so if you are in the room, you may not get straight answers – which is exactly what you *need*.

Probably the nicest gift that anyone can give you at this point of your business is a straight answer. It's much better to find out now – instead of after $50,000 of savings and debt – that your concept isn't going to fly.

Observation

Individual responses to surveys and focus groups are sometimes at odds with people's actual behavior. When you observe consumers in action in stores, at work, or at home, you can see how they buy or use a product. This gives you a more accurate picture of customers' usage habits and shopping patterns.

Strategies for Getting Straight Answers

Simple games that provide context and take the emotion out of the equation are great ways to get straight answers in market research. Whether you're doing a survey, an interview, or a focus group, try using these simple methods to get straight answers.

The Price is Right

Probably some of the best people to talk to about how to price a product or service are the game show participants of *The Price is Right*. The game show asks participants to guess the price of average household items such as laundry detergent, toothbrushes, dinette sets, and cars.

Interestingly, this simple game show is a better predictor of actual price points than our earlier questions (How much would you pay? How much would you charge?) The answers to these two different questions are hardly ever the same. In 99% of cases, Willingness to Accept (WTA) is far higher than the Willingness to Pay (WPA), meaning that one, or both, is wrong.

This is because both of these questions get our emotions involved – we're actively participating as the buyer or the seller in this hypothetical situation.

Willingness to Pay – "How much would you pay?" In this case, you are the buyer and this is the price you would be wiling to pay someone else. No one wants to pay a lot and everyone wants a deal, so participants generally report a lower than average price.

Willingness to Accept – "How much would you charge?" In this case you are the seller and this is the price you would charge.

Everyone wants to make a lot of money in their business, so participants generally report a higher than average price.

The best way to predict the best price is to take emotion out of it — **you're not the buyer or the seller**. You're just a person on a game show guessing prices!

Create a list of 10 offers — your offer and nine real offers of similar or related items and ask people to guess the prices. The nine real offers create a baseline. Does this person generally guess 25% higher? Adjust their guess of your offer accordingly. Use the price estimates to create a market-driven retail price for your offering.

Comparing 3 Offers

It's difficult sometimes to get good survey results or interview insights for a hypothetical offering. The more realistic the environment, the better.

One way to create a realistic situation is to put your offer in context. For instance, when you go to the grocery store, the store has multiple items — and you make *choices*. Most products and services are bought in the context of other products and services. Very rarely do stores carry one product with salespeople posted at the door asking, "Will you buy this or not?"

Using three large index cards, create three different offers for participants to compare. Make one of the offers your offer, along with two decoys. First, describe your offering, complete with price (for instance, the price from *The Price is Right* exercise), features, and details. If possible, sketch it out and make it visual. Do the same for two other complementary real-life or make-believe offerings.

For the best results, create six decoys and mix up the offers as much as possible. The more choices and the more rounds and participants, the more insight you will get into the minds of your potential customers.

Present the three cards to participants and ask them to rate each offer on a scale of one to five, one being "I would never buy this and can't think of one person who would" and five being "I would definitely buy this now – where can I get one?" After they've rated each offering, ask them *why* they chose that rating.

Is it too expensive? Do they need it? Is it missing an important feature?

Field Trials

Placing a new product in selected stores to test customer response under real-life selling conditions can help you make product modifications, adjust prices, or improve packaging. If you're going to be selling a new product in a store, try to establish a good relationship with local store owners and see if they might be willing to let you test out your product on their shelves to find the best price and packaging combination.

Online Field Trial: Testing response through ad clicks

If you're planning on selling products or services online, you're in luck – online ads are an easy way to conduct an online field trial.

By advertising your concept product or service online, you can measure how many clicks you will get when you actually launch your product. A Google Adwords (www.google.com/adwords) or Facebook Ads (www.facebook.com/ads) campaign might help.

If your audience is a business or professional audience, contact groups via LinkedIn, or create a LinkedIn Direct Ad targeted by industry, company, geography, job title, function, company size, etc (www.linkedin.com/directads/home).

Here's the concept. You are looking to target 18-22 year olds in Denver. Google provides geo-targeting by default in its Adwords interface, so you could just target Denver. However, if you want to get even more precise, Facebook Ads allows you to further narrow your target audience by geography, education, interests, keywords, and other personal information.

Before you create an ad campaign on Google, Facebook, LinkedIn or other online advertising network, you'll have to create a website to "sell" your product. This doesn't need to be an expensive or difficult task – in Chapter 8, there are three different ways to create your own awesome website on a budget.

Create a website with your pricing information, product details, etc., and a checkout button. What we're really interested to see is how many people click on the Checkout button. Install Google Analytics on your site and track how many users click on the Checkout page.

Beware: It is ILLEGAL to take anyone's credit card information or make a *sale* if you do not have a product ready to ship. This is called false advertising and it's a serious offense. Instead, on the "checkout" page of your website, let your potential customers know that your product is not ready to ship quite yet and encourage them to check back later. Better yet, have them fill out a request to be notified when the product is ready.

Create multiple offers, for instance – three different price points. Check to see the difference in click volume for the different prices and checkouts.

Get a mentor

Regardless of the business model you pursue, proven or new-to-the-world, make sure you're not solving an imaginary problem. The best way to find out is to talk to a business mentor, an industry expert, and a potential customer about your business concept.

Mentors can help you think through the nuts and bolts of your business. Industry experts can tell you what's really happening in the market and where the real opportunities are.   A potential customer will tell you what they're looking for and what price point is reasonable.

Mentors are easier to find than you might think. SCORE is a network of retired business executives who volunteer their time to help entrepreneurs. SCORE is funded by the U.S. Small Business Administration (SBA) and helps entrepreneurs secure SBA small business loans.

SCORE mentors come from all industry backgrounds and most have either served as executives at large companies or have owned a business. These mentors can help you write your business plan and build your financial projections.

The organization has chapters in almost every city. To find a mentor in your city, visit www.score.org.

5   How to Finance a Startup

"If God only gave me a clear sign, like making a large deposit in my name at a Swiss bank."
— Woody Allen

Why Startup Finance is So Important

According to the SBA, over 50% of small businesses fail in the first five years. The interesting point is *why*. Four of the top 10 reasons for business failures are related to financing, which is why it's so important to understand this aspect of entrepreneurship well.

1. Lack of experience
2. *Insufficient capital (money)*
3. Poor location
4. Poor inventory management
5. *Over-investment in fixed assets*
6. *Poor credit arrangements*
7. *Personal use of business funds*
8. Unexpected growth
9. Competition
10. Low sales

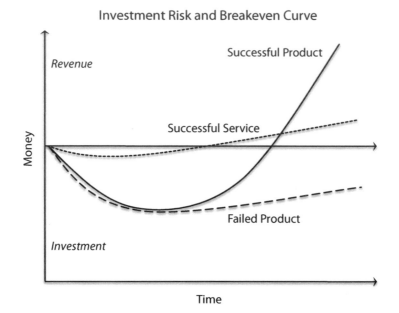

According to Babson College, the preeminent school for entrepreneurship in the U.S., the average cost to start a business today is about $65,000.

Generally speaking, the cost is higher for product companies than for service companies. But regardless of the type of company, know this: -Startups are cash hogs and time is your enemy. The graph above shows how money is spent and earned over time in a startup and how long it takes to break even. In no other business than a startup is the relationship between time and money so apparent. The faster you can bring revenue in the door, the less investment capital you have to raise.

How the Average Startup is Funded

By far, the number one source of financing for a startup is the entrepreneur. About **76%** of companies are personally financed by the entrepreneur through savings and personal debt such as credit cards and home equity loans.

When most people think of how startups are financed, they think of equity investors. This is not necessarily the case. According to the Federal Reserve's Survey of Small Business Finances, of the funding received by new businesses (less than two years old), approximately half (52%) is debt and half (48%) is equity.

At the same time, when we think of equity investors and lenders, we generally think of banks, accredited angel investors and venture capital investors. It turns out that much of this financing comes from informal sources such as friends and family. In fact, about **23%** of startups receive some kind of support from friends and family. Informal investors might also take the form of a local business owner. These informal sources make loans and investments in roughly equal proportions. In a survey of informal investors, about 45% said their investments were equity investments and 55% took the form of debt.

Surprisingly, these informal investors are not as wealthy as we would think – and their investments tend to be small. About 40% of informal investors have an annual income of less than $50,000 and more than half of their investments were less than $10,000. Just 23% of investments were more than $20,000 and only 1% was more than $200,000.

This is not to say that informal investors are not savvy business people. Probably the best example of one of these informal investors is Ian McGlinn, the owner of a garage in Sussex, England, who invested about $17,000 for a 50% stake in a company called the Body Shop. The company now has 2,400 stores in 61 countries. Not bad for a friendly investment.

For early stage companies that do receive some form of formal equity investment, the source is usually angel investors ($25,000-$1 million) – not venture capital investors. Only one in a thousand companies receive some sort of venture capital investment – and the ones that do receive venture capital are usually at a later stage (12 months to 5 years after the start of the company).

Angel investors and venture capital investors still play an important role in the start-up world. While angel investors only account for 3.6% of small-business financing and VCs only account for 1.9% of small-business financing, the success of companies backed by formal investors is notably better than those that are not. Their advice, networks, and financial investments have built companies Apple, Google, Facebook, Genentech, and many others.

In this chapter we will outline 14 sources of capital for startups – from self-funded businesses to venture capital and SBA loans. We'll examine the factors driving your decision: your credit, type of business, amount of capital needed and time to break even.

We will also explore ways to **keep your cost of capital low, maintain ownership, and manage your risk.**

Identify your Start-up Costs

You will incur a lot of expenses when you launch your company, so make sure you have a good handle on all the costs before you start. Let's determine the amount of capital you will really need at startup.

Some of these expenses will be one-time expenses, such as:
- Website
- Office furniture
- Equipment purchases
- Security Deposits

Others will become recurring expenses, like:
- Rent
- Salaries
- Advertising
- Internet
- Utilities
- Insurance

Before you can determine whether you have the personal financial capability to finance your company – or approach lenders or investors – you must have a complete, itemized budget of your start-up costs and recurring costs. This is your maximum downside – the amount you stand to lose if things don't work out.

If this business is your only source of income, make sure you factor in your living expenses. It may be months before you have any paying customers, and it's important to be proactive. Make sure to have more cash on hand than you think you will need. It always takes twice as much to start up and twice as long to break even than you expect.

The following worksheet details common costs at startup. Use this to estimate your start-up costs.

Startup cost calculator

		One-Time Start-Up Costs		
	1	Purchase price or downpayment if buying a business	$0.00	
	2	Office furniture	$2,000.00	
	3	Computer hardware and software	$2,500.00	
	4	Setup, installation and consulting fees	$0.00	
	5	Business cards and stationery (design & printing)	$700.00	
	6	Decorating and remodeling	$0.00	
	7	Fixtures, counters, equipment & Installation	$0.00	
	8	Starting inventory, raw materials, tools, etc.	$0.00	
	9	Deposits with public utilities	$0.00	
	10	Legal and other professional fees	$500.00	
	11	Business licenses and permits	$0.00	
	12	Advertising and promotion for opening	$2,000.00	
	13	Signage	$0.00	
	14	Rent & security deposit (often equals 3 months rent)	$0.00	
	15	Operating Cash	$0.00	
	16	Website	$5,000.00	
	17	Other	$0.00	
	18	Other	$0.00	
	19	Other	$0.00	
	20	Other	$0.00	
		Subtotal	$12,700.00	
		Monthly Expenses		
	17	Salary of owner-manager (amount you need to pay yourself)	$5,000.00	
	18	All other salaries, wages, & commissions	$0.00	
	19	Payroll taxes or self-employment tax	$0.00	
	20	Rent	$0.00	
	21	Equipment lease payments	$0.00	
	22	Advertising (print, broadcast and Internet)	$300.00	
	23	Postage & shipping costs	$0.00	
	24	Supplies (inks, toners, labels, paper goods, etc.)	$100.00	
	25	Telephone	$200.00	
	26	Utilities	$0.00	
	27	Internet connection	$50.00	
	28	Website hosting and maintenance	$20.00	
	29	General business insurance	$0.00	
	30	Business vehicle insurance	$0.00	
	31	Health insurance	$100.00	
	32	Interest & principal on loans & credit cards	$0.00	
	33	Inventory, raw materials, parts	$0.00	
	34	Legal and other professional fees	$0.00	
	35	Franchise fee	$0.00	
	36	Other	$0.00	
	37	Other	$0.00	
	38	Other	$0.00	
	39	Other	$0.00	
		Subtotal	$5,770.00	
		Calculate total start-up funds		
	40	Estimate the number of months needed to find customers and get established	4	
	41	**Monthly expense for months**	$23,080.00	
	42	**One time start-up expense**	$12,700.00	
	43	**Total start-up costs**	**$35,780.00**	

Factors Driving Available Sources of Capital

Now, depending on the following four factors, your business will qualify for different sources of capital.

- Amount of capital needed
- Length of time before capital can be repaid (lump sum or in payments)
- Risk of the business model
- Potential upside (profits) of the business model

The answers to all four of these factors are driven by the type of business you are starting.

Lifestyle company (for example, a "Four-Hour Workweek" business): This kind of business is designed to create only as much profit as you need in order to have a comfortable lifestyle. A lifestyle company requires little to no capital in order to get started ($5,000-$25,000) and is usually financed by the entrepreneur using personal savings.

Franchise (for example, McDonald's or Massage Envy): Most franchises require a good amount of financing at startup ($100,000 - $1 million), but are generally easier to finance with debt since franchises are established business models. Banks can be assured that a well-located McDonald's franchise will earn a certain amount in profits, compared with an untested restaurant concept. Part of the start-up expense of a franchise is the franchise fee – the cost to license the brand name, operating procedures, and other franchise benefits.

Bricks & mortar establishment (for example, a retail store or a restaurant): Construction and build-out of any physical establishment can be costly and these types of firms generally require a good amount of financing to start up ($100,000 – $1 million). These firms may qualify for debt financing since there's collateral such as real estate and equipment, but will likely need additional equity financing if the concept is new and untested. Because of the inherent risk of new retail and restaurant concepts, equity investors and SBA lenders are the typical sources of financing. When the location is leased, the landlord may pay for the build-out of the interior of the location and roll that cost into the monthly rent. In this case, the landlord is also a source of start-up financing.

Social enterprise or nonprofit (for example, Kiva.org or the Salvation Army): These firms are generally funded through donations and grants from foundations or governments – not debt or equity investors. If you're a social entrepreneur that is more mission driven than profit driven, you may want to consider organizing as a nonprofit.

Service business or consultancy (for example, a landscaping company or an accounting firm): Low barriers to entry and minimal start-up costs make it possible for most service businesses and consulting firms to bootstrap their startup – selling their services to clients and growing organically. These firms usually require very little start-up financing and are financed by the entrepreneur, friends and family, and in some cases, a small amount of debt financing.

Product company (for example, a line of clothing, a toy, or a tool): The design, manufacturing, packaging, and delivery of any product is a costly endeavor, so most product companies require a good amount of financing at startup ($50,000 - $500,000). The set-up costs for manufacturing alone (molds, designs, tools, etc.) can cost upward of $50,000 and most contract manufacturers require a minimum order to make the job profitable.

Because these firms have very little collateral for lenders, debt financing can be tricky. The inherent risk of a new product and the high cost of startup mean that friends and family, SBA lenders, and equity investors are the likely sources of financing. Lenders will look for low-risk plans and collateral, and equity investors will look for high growth potential.

Some products, like T-shirts, are benefiting from variable production technology, where centralized contract manufacturers produce the order only once it's been ordered online, essentially creating zero-inventory product companies, requiring little to no financing and making bootstrapping possible for these product companies.

Internet-based (for example, an online store, a blog, or a Web application): Depending on the type of firm (ecommerce, content-based, software application), Internet-based companies can require as little as $5,000 and as much as $500,000 to start up. The primary driver of cost is the development of the Website or Web application. The vast majority of these firms require very little capital to start up ($5,000-$25,000). Generally, they are financed by the entrepreneur, friends and family, or occasionally, through a small amount of debt financing. In some cases, mid-sized applications that cost $25,000-$100,000 to build can be financed fully or partially with sweat equity agreements with web developers. Larger web applications that have unproven business models but high growth potential are usually financed by equity investors.

High-tech company that IPOs (goes public) in five to 10 years (for example, Google or Genentech): These firms are mostly financed with equity investments: first from the entrepreneur and friends and family, then angel investors, then venture capital investors. These firms generally have a high-risk profile at startup, making them unattractive to lenders.

Theory

Money often costs too much. ~*Ralph Waldo Emerson*

Capital is a resource like labor, property, or equipment, and it has a cost like any other resource. The goal is to **find the lowest cost of capital for your startup**, given the amount of capital needed, the risk potential of the business model, and your personal financial situation.

Regardless of the source, keep in mind that **outside money isn't free**.

Debt

When capital is borrowed, **the cost of capital is the interest rate**. An interest rate could be as low as 0% for some credit cards (limited to six to 12 months) or as high as 20% in some cases.

The debt could be *secured* with an asset such as a home or property, garnering a lower interest rate, but also risking loss of the asset if the loan payments cannot be made. For example, a home equity loan is secured by your home. In this case your home is the *collateral*. This potentially allows you to borrow $25,000-$100,000 at an interest rate as low as mortgage rates (5-8%) – but you risk losing your home if things don't work out and you can't pay back the loan.

The debt could be *unsecured*, limiting the amount of capital that can be borrowed to about $25,000 and garnering a higher interest rate (10-14%). A credit card is a form of unsecured debt. If you fail to make the payments, Visa doesn't start taking your assets, but your credit score will plummet when they file your late payments with the credit bureaus.

In some cases, debt can be *guaranteed* by an outside party such as the Small Business Administration, which guarantees 50-90% of the risk of the loan and pays the loan in the case of *default* (failure to pay or otherwise abide by the terms of the loan agreement).

Debt is considered a *non-dilutive* form of capital, meaning that you do not give up ownership of your company.

Equity

When capital is raised in the form of equity, **the cost of the capital is the forgone percentage of ownership**. In the case of a startup, this could be 5% or 75%. In the classic example of a technology company that has a patent and an idea for how to build a software platform, the founder could give up 50% of the company (and control of the company) for a $1 million investment.

Equity is considered a *dilutive* form of capital, meaning that you give up a percentage of ownership in order to raise equity.

It's also important to note that as you give up ownership of the company, you also give up *control*. Formal investors generally require a seat on the board of the company, which controls all major financial and strategic decisions – including whether you should be the CEO.

The 14 Sources of Cash for Startups

	Non-Dilutive		Dilutive
Internal	Revenue	Life Savings	
	Lease Terms	Payment Terms	Sweat Equity
External	**Grants**	**Debt**	**Equity**
	SBIR/High tech R&D	SBA *guaranteed* line of credit/loan - 7m microloan	Friends & Family
	Minority Businesses	- 7a - 504	Angel investors
	Economic Development	Home Equity	Venture capital
	Nonprofit/Social entrepreneurship	Peer-to-Peer Credit cards	

The chart above details 14 different potential sources of cash for startups. Let's take a look at these sources in order of preference.

The best source of cash for your business is revenue (sales). Some service businesses are able to finance their business almost entirely on revenue. Take a landscaping business, for example. A 12-year-old boy might start a revenue-financed business simply by advertising his lawn-mowing service and renting or borrowing equipment until he's mowed enough lawns that he can afford to buy a commercial mower. This is bootstrapping at its best.

The second is grant funding, but very few for-profit companies qualify for grants. For-profit startups that do qualify are either extremely high tech (grants from the Small Business Innovative Research Program) or part of a local economic development effort.

Grants (whether federal grants or private foundation grants) most commonly go to non-profit organizations. We will not go into non-profits in detail, but if you are a social entrepreneur and more mission-driven than profit-driven you should investigate whether grant funding is available for your particular mission, and if so, consider organizing as a non-profit.

The third source is your personal savings. Given that the average cost to start a business is $65,000, you may not have that amount of cash on hand. However, investors, banks, and even family will want to know how much "skin in the game" – in other words, how much of your own money you've invested in your company.

The fourth is a tie between sweat equity, SBA loans, and friends and family. Sweat equity agreements are good options for startups whose major expenses are professional services such as developers or designers.

SBA loans are excellent resources for startups because they are generally low-interest loans that limit the entrepreneur's overall risk exposure. SBA loans also usually come with a start-up checklist, templates, and a SCORE mentor – all great resources.

Friends and family are great sources for investment or loans because they care about the entrepreneur. When parents, grandparents, and close friends make informal investments, their interest is both in the personal happiness and growth of the entrepreneur in addition to the business opportunity.

But don't get into a business relationship with your family and friends lightly: If things go wrong, the downside may be irreparable harm to the relationships that matter most. Make sure you explain the risks of your business clearly and find out what your friends and family expect in return. Managing expectations by having a plan and an agreement in place will save you headaches and heartache if things don't work out as planned.

Personal forms of debt such as home equity loans, credit cards, peer-to-peer loans are all worthwhile options to investigate, but come with specific caveats. Despite their attractive low-interest rates, home equity loans put not only your business but also your home at risk, so make sure that you can afford to make every payment no matter what —or you'll be facing foreclosure. Credit cards are a fast form of cash and many cards come with a 0% introductory rate. But after the first six to 12 months, you'll be paying a really high-interest rate. Peer-to-peer loans, which have been around for just over two years, are an interesting and potentially lower-interest alternative to credit cards, but are still fairly untested.

Formal investments from angel and venture investors come with a fundamentally higher price tag. Angel and venture investors require a healthy financial return, which means less ownership – and control – for you. Formal investors have high standards and high expectations. Taking a significant investment from an active, formal investor means that you will report progress and problems to them much like you would report to a boss. The performance of your company —and your own performance – is constantly on their mind. The good news is that when a large, powerful venture capital fund makes an investment in your company, they not only provide investment capital, but advice and high-level connections as well.

Strategy

Our strategy will be two-fold:
- Minimize your downside (risk)
- Maximize your upside (profit)

What drives an owner's decision when raising debt or equity?

Debt:
- Interest rate (minimize) –This will be based largely on your credit score.
- Amount borrowed – You pay interest on what you borrow, so only borrow as much as you need.
- Term – Longer terms mean lower monthly payments, but more in total interest paid.
- Secured vs. Unsecured – This refers to whether there's collateral (such as your house or car) that may be taken by the lender if you *default*.
- Guarantee –Who will pay the loan if things don't go well?

Equity:
- Pre-money valuation (maximize) –This is the value of your company before investors invest.
- Money raised –The more money you raise, the more ownership you give up, so only raise as much as you need.
- Percentage ownership –Maximize your ownership (based on pre-money valuation and money raised).
- Control (either by ownership or membership interest) –You lose control of the company if you do not have more than 50% of the vote (governed by the Operating Agreement and other agreements).

Debt vs. Equity

Case Study: The $20,000 iPhone App

One of the thousands of business plans I've had the pleasure of reading was for a simple iPhone app that was created by two young women finishing their MBAs. The app was extremely practical and easy to use; in fact, similar successful apps existed on the Android and Blackberry mobile platforms and were performing well, but iPhone developers had yet to launch a similar app. For purposes of this case study, we'll call the app the UltraApp.

UltraApp pitched to my group and explained the cost of development, the sale price of the app on the app store ($2), and the sales volumes of similar apps (10,000-1 million).

Based on their up-front cost of $20,000 for development and launch marketing, it would take 10,000 downloads just to break even.

The two students were living on the meager salaries of their summer internships. While their parents might have been able to help at another time, they were already paying tuition expenses and weren't in a position to make a $20,000 loan.

The two founders were at a critical decision point. Should they get investors or get a loan?

Equity

Investors look for big upside, so they would need to be convinced that this one app was going to do well on the iPhone app store. Formal investors such as venture funds were unlikely to get interested – a $20,000 investment was too small to be worth their time, especially when the legal bill for the deal was going to be as much as the investment itself. Informal investors might take a look, though. The question was this: How much ownership would an informal investor want for the company?

Let's say the investor wants a third of the company. That means that the implied pre-money valuation is $40,000. Do the students think their idea and work to date is worth $40,000?

		Ownership
Pre-money valuation	$40,000	67% Founders
Investment	$20,000	33% Investor
Post money	$60,000	

The founders know that by giving up 33% of the company, they also give up 33% of the profits. Over the next three years, they believe that their app will be downloaded 50,000 times per year at $2 per download, or $100,000 in profits each year. This means that they will give up $33,000 in profits each year, or $100,000 over three years. This is a pretty steep price to pay for short-term cash.

The investor will get five times his money back over the course of three years – over a 150% return, so he'll be happy. After examining their calculations, the two friends consider offering a smaller equity stake by increasing the pre-money valuation of their company.

By keeping the investor in a minority position, the founders will control two of the three seats on the board, maintaining solid control of their company.

Debt

Banks look for zero risk that their loan will be paid back – with interest – whether the business succeeds or not. So, they look at the inherent risk of the business plan and the ability of the owners to pay if things don't work out.

Currently enrolled in an MBA program, neither of the founders owns a house or has much in the way of assets that can be borrowed against or used as collateral. However, because the size of the loan is so small (under $25,000), the women have plenty of options.

Credit cards are the fastest form of debt, but the founders need cash to pay their iPhone developer – and the cash withdrawal fees on credit cards are steep. Also, each student would need to take on an additional $10,000 in credit card debt and neither is sure how long it will take to pay off the balance. Their credit is good now, but not high enough to qualify for the 0% introductory rates, so they're looking at credit card interest rates of around 10%. Surely, there's a better rate out there.

Their second option is an SBA loan. After talking to their local Small Business Development Center (SBDC), they find that they can borrow up to $25,000 at a 7.5% interest rate over a seven-year term with no prepayment penalty. On a $20,000 loan, this means that the monthly payment on their loan would be about $300 per month and they would pay about $5,800 in interest over the life of the loan.

If things work out, the students believe that they will break even in 12 months and can pay back the SBA loan. At the end of 12 months, they'll pay the outstanding balance on the loan (about $17,700), effectively spending only $1,400 total on interest. If things don't work out, their maximum downside is a $300-a-month loan payment for seven years – about $150 a month each. With a seven-year term, low monthly payments, low-interest rate, and no prepayment penalty, this loan gives the students maximum flexibility.

The loan is going to take about two weeks to process and requires a business plan, financial projections, and a personal financial statement complete with credit check. The loan is unsecured and made to the business – and if they go forward with the application, the partners will be paired with a SCORE mentor who will help them with the loan application and business plan and any questions they might have in the future. The women decide that the SBA loan is a pretty good option.

A third option for the UltraApp partners is a peer-to-peer loan with Prosper or Lending Club, which allow borrowers to post loan requests online of up to $25,000. While the interest rate on this loan is slightly higher than the SBA loan (about 9%) and while the term is only three years, there are very few requirements – just a credit check and a paragraph describing the business. On a $20,000 loan, the monthly payment would be about $635 and they would pay $2,900 in total interest. For a slightly higher interest rate (10%), the women can get a longer term – a five-year loan from Lending Club. This would lower their monthly payment to $425 per month and they would pay about $5,500 in total interest. The two friends already have a business plan and financial projections, so the requirements are not an issue for them. The main issue is going to be the monthly payment if things don't go as planned. They decide that the SBA loan is the best option for them.

Think Creatively: Sweat Equity

Another option for the students is to strike an agreement with their iPhone developer. The cost of development represents about 80% of their budget, or $16,000. The other $4,000 is needed for advertising and marketing. If the iPhone developer agrees to a

Sweat Equity deal, the question is: How much ownership will he want?

If we use the same equation and same pre-money valuation of $40,000 from above, the iPhone developer would get 29% of the company.

		Ownership
Pre-money valuation	$40,000	71% Founders
Sweat Equity	$16,000	29% Sweat equity owner
Post money	$56,000	

		Maximum	How long it takes	Cost	Probability of success
Grants	SBIR	$150,000-$500,000	6 months	Free	10%-30%
Debt	SBA 7m	$35,000	15-30 days	8-13%	50%-85%
	SBA 7a	$2,000,000	30-60 days	5-9%	50%-85%
	SBA 7a Express	$100,000	15-30 days	5-9%	50%-85%
	SBA CDC 504	$1,500,000	30-60 days	5-9%	50%-85%
	Home Equity	$25,000-$100,000	15-60 days	3-7%	
	Credit Cards	$25,000	1-7 days	0-23%	
	Peer to Peer	$25,000	14 days	7-18%	15%-25%
Equity	Angel Investors	$50,000-$1,000,000	3-12 months	20-50%	0.01%-5%
	Venture Capital	$1,000,000-$5,000,000	6-18 months	20-50%	0.01%

Term	Advantages	Disadvantages
No term	Significant maximum, non-dilutive.	Takes 1 month to prepare application. Awards are announced 6 months after.
7 years	Debt is guaranteed by the SBA. Fast and easy application process. Reasonable interest rates, long term, low monthly payment. Comes with a business coach.85% of loan guaranteed.	
10-25 years	Same advantages as above.	
10-25 years	Same advantages as above. 50% of loan guaranteed.	
10-25 years	Same advantages as above. 50% of loan guaranteed.	
15 years	Low interest rates. Option to do revolving HELOC or loan.	Home is collateral for the loan.
6-12 months for 0%, or revolving	Unsecured, revolving line of credit.	Hard inquiry, high interest rates after introductory rate.
3 years	Unsecured. Soft credit inquiry.	Short term. High monthly payments.
5-10 year horizon	Bring expertise and network as well as capital.	Can take a year to raise equity from angel investors.
5-10 year horizon	Bring expertise and network as well as capital.	Can take over a year to raise equity from VCs.

Tactics

Other Sources of Financing

Payment terms with Vendors & Customers – Working on the terms of your payments to vendors and from customers can be another way to finance a company, especially if there's a big selling opportunity for vendors in the future or if there's a specialized product/service that customers really need. And in some cases, vendors or customers are potential equity investors.

For product companies, one financing strategy is to work on your cash conversion cycle – the number of days between when you have to pay your vendors and when your customers pay you.

For instance, let's say you have a new product design and a manufacturer all lined up. You show the design to a potential customer and they love it; they'll order 1,000 units at $200 per unit, or $200,000. The only problem is that the product costs $100 up front to manufacture, meaning that you need to come up with $100,000 fast in order to manufacture the order. Not only that, but the customer is a big company – and they take 90 days to pay an invoice. Meanwhile, your manufacturer requires 100% up front payment from new customers. This means that you would need $100,000 for 90 days. How will you finance it?

First, you need a signed purchase order from your customer with terms that protect you if your customer fails to pay. Second, you need a firm price quote from your manufacturer. Now, you need to get creative. You have four choices:
   1. Get the customer to pay up front (offer a better price, bonus units, etc.)

2. Get the vendor to accept a 90-day term instead of paying up front (offer a better price, interest rate over the 90 days, etc.)
3. Do a combination of the two – get your customer to pay in 60 days and your manufacturer to give you 30 days
4. Find a bank to finance the $100,000 purchase order for 90 day

Landlord investment – In the case of retail stores and restaurants, construction and build out is the largest start-up expense and the landlord may be the best source of financing because. Tenant Improvements (TI) or Tenant Allowance (TA) can be increased in the lease (and likely built into the cost per square foot of the rent), in a way, financing the cost of building.

When building out a bricks-and-mortar location, make sure your commercial real estate broker understands your overall financing strategy and that you want to include as much of the construction cost as possible in the lease itself.

Debt

Over half of small business owners have some form of debt financing. We will cover several sources of debt financing, including friends and family, SBA loans, peer-to-peer online loans, credit cards, and home equity loans.

Borrowing from Friends & Family

About a quarter of all entrepreneurs receive some kind of support – whether it's a grant, equity investment, or a loan – from friends or family members. Friends and family are generally interested in your well-being as well as a financial return, so in many cases, an investment or a loan is a win-win. But before you jump into family financing, make sure that you've considered all the ramifications. For instance, how will Thanksgiving dinner go if you're late on your loan payment? In bringing your friends and family into your business as investors or lenders, you may find yourself one day having tough business conversations with the people you love.

Start off with a thorough discussion about the risks of your business plan and be honest about your chances for success.
What will happen if the business fails?
What will happen if the business is wildly successful?

If you decide to go forward, put your agreement in writing. It may be years before you revisit this discussion and you want to have an accurate account of the agreement for everyone's reference. If you decide to do a loan, Lending Karma and Virgin Money have great online tools that administer friends and family loan agreements and payment schedules online – making it easier to keep track of your loan.

Another important reason to document your agreement is for estate-planning purposes. In the case of parents and grandparents, loans and investments that go undocumented could cause family strife later on. If Grandma made a forgivable loan two years ago, but has since passed away, you may find yourself arguing with your closest relatives at an emotional time. Money is the No. 1 killer of relationships– even among families – so document everything.

Peer-to-peer lending sites such as VirginMoney.com and LendingKarma.com can help you craft a loan agreement and payment schedule, and they can track your loan online. These sites ensure that everyone's interests – and the relationship – are protected.

Borrowing from Banks and Other Formal Lenders

Before you apply for a loan, you need to determine your credit score so that you know what the lender will see. If there are any inaccuracies on your report, you can take care of them before you apply for a loan.

There are three major credit reporting bureaus – Equifax, Experian, and TransUnion – and each may have slightly different information about your credit history. If your score is low, your best bet is to pull a three-bureau report and get all the details. FreeCreditReport.com allows you to check all three credit bureaus, ensuring that you have a complete list of all negative reports concerning your credit so that you can resolve any issues and increase your credit score before you apply for a loan.

Why Credit Score Matters

Let's say you and a friend are each applying for a $50,000 loan that will be paid back over 10 years. Your friend's credit score is 800 (excellent) and your score is 600 (pretty low).

The bank offers your friend a 5% interest rate and offers you a 15% interest rate. A $50,000 loan at 5% interest over 10 years costs $13,639 in interest. A $50,000 loan at 15% interest over 10 years costs $46,802 in interest.

That means that you'll pay almost $35,000 more in interest than your friend just for being a higher risk to the bank.

Do Your Research – and Apply to <u>One</u> Lender

Each time you apply for credit, a lender will pull your credit report. This is known as a hard inquiry. Multiple inquiries will lower your credit score, so make sure to do your research first, evaluate all your options, make your selection, and apply to one lender.

Apply for a Loan While You are Still Employed

There's an old saying: "Banks only give loans to people who don't need the money." In some ways, this is true. Banks don't want to make a loan if there's a risk that it won't be paid back. This is called default risk – and banks do everything they can to minimize this risk. If you can, apply for a loan while you are still employed. This will help reassure the banks that you're a good risk because they know that you have a salary and will be able to pay the loan back regardless.

Traditional Business Loans

According to the SBA, 50% of businesses fail within the first five years, so startups are a bad risk for most traditional banks. Business lenders generally require two years of operating history, so it's rare to see a bank make a loan to a startup that is not an SBA guaranteed loan.

Small Business Administration (SBA) Loans

The Small Business Administration was created by Congress in 1953 to help Americans start businesses. The SBA provides loan guarantees as well as mentors and advice to small businesses. Most large banks such as Wells Fargo, US Bank, Huntington Bank, PNC Bank, and JP Morgan Chase are SBA lenders, taking business loan applications and working with the SBA to put together the loan.

There are plenty of myths and misconceptions about the SBA, so let's dispel those right away. Many people associate government programs with red tape and long lead times. The good news is that this is not necessarily the case with the Small Business Administration. SBA loans are processed in about the same amount of time and require the same documentation as regular business loans. Smaller loans can be processed in as little as 15-30 days.

The SBA itself does not make loans, rather it *guarantees* loans made to startups and small businesses that traditional banks deem too risky. This means that if a business defaults on an SBA loan, the SBA will cover the loss for the bank, which makes it less risky for the bank to lend in the first place. Regular commercial banks process the loan applications, do the underwriting, and present the loans for approval to the SBA. The SBA then reviews the application and decides whether it will grant the business a guarantee. Typically, the SBA will guarantee 75%-85% of the loan value. If the SBA grants the guarantee, the lender will then administer the loan.

The SBA's maximum guarantee is $1 million and the total amount that you can borrow under the SBA program is $2 million. The interest rate is determined by the lender (and your credit score) and is generally 2-5% above the current *Prime Rate* (base interest rate), depending on the loan program. In the case of startups, the SBA requires that at least a third (33%) of the total project cost is contributed by the borrower. To estimate the interest rate, find the posted WSJ Prime Rate online or in the *Wall Street Journal* and add 2-5% to that rate.

The lender and SBA will require a good amount of information, including:

1. A business plan
2. Your personal financial statements
3. Your business financial statements (if already in business)
4. What collateral is available to secure the loan
5. Assumptions used in your financial projections
6. Your resume
7. Pro-forma profit and loss projections showing what the business would look like if the loan were granted

The term of the loan varies depending on the purpose of the loan. Loans used to purchase real estate or make improvements to property have a longer term – an amortization period of up to 25 years. Loans used for working capital have a shorter term – up to 10 years.

There are three types of SBA loans: the 7(a) – the most common and most flexible type of SBA loan, the 7(m) microloan, and the 504 fixed-asset loan.

SBA 7(a) loans are the most basic and most commonly used type of loan and allow you to borrow as little as $25,000 and as much as $2 million. They are also the most flexible, since financing can be guaranteed for a variety of general business purposes. That includes working capital, machinery and equipment, furniture and fixtures, land and building (including purchase, renovation and new construction), leasehold improvements, and debt refinancing (under special conditions). Loan maturity is up to 10 years for working capital and generally up to 25 years for fixed assets.

These loans are issued by commercial banks, but are regulated by the SBA and lend up to $2 million. SBA guarantees up to 85% percent of loans up to $150,000 and 75% of loans above $150,000. Smaller 7(a) loans (under $100,000) can be processed as SBA Express loans. These loans are reviewed in 36 hours (hence "Express") and the SBA may guarantee up to 50% of the loan value.

The 7(a) loan guarantee is perfect for businesses that require more options for their loans and are having trouble getting funding through traditional lenders. This program offers more flexibility and, unlike the microloan 7(m), can be used to pay off your debts and acquire property for your business. You can also use your 7(a) loan for working capital or to purchase supplies, equipment, and furniture.

SBA 7(m) microloan is the most popular loan for home based businesses and is targeted at very small and start-up companies to purchase computers, equipment and materials required to launch a business. You may borrow as little as $5,000 and as much as $35,000 for up to six years. You can use this money in a variety of ways, such as purchasing needed inventory to run your business, buying necessary supplies or furniture, getting the computer equipment that you need, or for working capital. However, you will not be able to use this loan to pay off any existing debts or to purchase land or real estate for your home-based business.

Loan terms vary according to the size of the loan, the planned use of funds, the requirements of the intermediary lender, and the needs of the small-business borrower. The maximum term allowed for a microloan is six years. Interest rates vary, depending on the lender, but are generally 8-13%.

SBA CDC/504 loan is a long-term financing tool for economic development within a community. The 504 Program provides small businesses requiring "bricks and mortar" financing with long-term, fixed-rate financing to acquire major fixed assets for expansion or modernization. The Certified Development Company (CDC) 504 Loan Plan is primarily for larger businesses that require a great deal of money to purchase real estate or expensive equipment. The maximum loan size is $1.5 million unless the project is part of a public policy goal (maximum $2 million).

The CDC 504 Loan Plan is more complicated than the first two loans offered by the SBA. The business owner typically provides 10% of the equity for the purchase, another lender covers 50%, and the 504 loan will cover the remaining 40%. It's most often used to purchase real estate for businesses that are likely to increase the level of employment at the company. The guarantee value may be as high as 90% of the appraised value of the property.

What Are the Chances of Getting an SBA Loan?

While the SBA doesn't publish much data regarding applications and denials, Nara Mijid of Central Connecticut State University was able to uncover some fascinating insights about small-business lending in her survey of small businesses. She found that the average probability of denial is about 15% - meaning that about 85% of all SBA loans are approved. However, this number includes both startup and non-startup small-business loans.

Also, keep in mind that SBA loan applications are pre-screened by lenders – and in the case of startups, are usually crafted with the help of SCORE mentors and other intermediaries. It may take several revisions to your business plan and hours of mentoring before your application is SBA-ready.

SBA lending in 2009 was down 30% nationally compared with the previous year. The SBA program is dependent on commercial banks, so during tough economic times, SBA loans are like any other type of loan: hard to get.

SBA loan volumes vary greatly bank to bank and region to region. Below is a chart that details five of the top 30 SBA lenders in the country and their total SBA loan volume in millions over two years. Each of these banks made between 500 and 2,000 SBA loans across the country in 2009. Each vary greatly in terms of their local loan volumes, so when looking for a local SBA lender, call your local SBA office and find out which banks in your local area participate in each SBA program and offer the type of loan you're looking for.

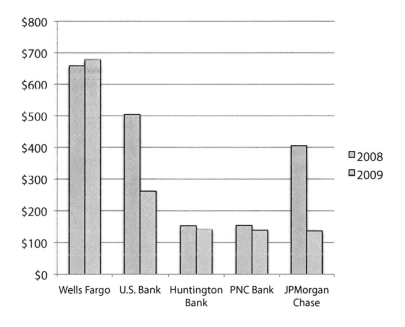

SBA Loans (in Millions)

Credit Cards

In some rare cases, credit cards can be used for extremely low rates of interest for extremely short periods of time. The absolute only reason you would use credit cards to finance your company:

- You have great credit (720+ needed in order to qualify for the 0% rate).
- You need less than the limit offered ($5,000-$25,000).
- You can afford to pay it all back whether it works out or not in six-12 months.
- You have a 0% APR card (six-12 months).

It's very rare that a startup can pay off any debt within the first year of operations. But when short-term cash flow is an issue (as it is for product companies in the 30-90 days between paying vendors and getting paid by customers), this mode of financing can play an important role.

It's also important to note that credit cards are personal loans and carrying a high balance over a long period will lower your credit score, making other loans such as mortgages and auto loans more expensive in the future.

In most cases, though, there's a better alternative. The graph below shows the difference between a 7% SBA loan and a 12 month, 0% introductory interest credit card. After the 12-month introductory period, the interest rate jumps to 18%, creating high monthly payments and a large interest expense that could have been avoided.

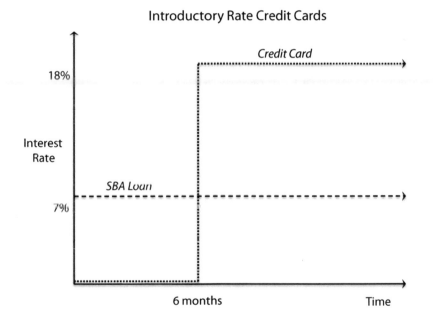

Introductory Rate Credit Cards

Home Equity Loans or Lines of Credit

A home equity loan allows you to borrow money using your home's equity as collateral. There are two types of home equity debt: home equity loans and home equity lines of credit, also known as HELOCs.

A home equity loan is sometimes referred to as a second mortgage because it is secured by your property, just like your mortgage. Home equity loans and lines of credit are usually repaid in a shorter period than first mortgages. Most mortgages are 30-year mortgages. Most equity loans and lines of credit have a repayment period of 15 years, although they can be as short as five and as long as 30 years.

Collateral is property that you pledge as a guarantee that you will repay a debt. If you don't repay the debt, the lender can take your collateral and sell it to get the money back. With a home equity loan or line of credit, you pledge your home as collateral, which means you will lose the home and be forced to move out if you don't repay the debt.

Home equity is the difference between **how much the home is worth** and **how much you owe on the mortgage**.

To find out how much your home is worth, check out Zillow.com. Zillow uses recent sales in your area to determine what your house might sell for today. An alternative to Zillow is your local county auditor, the property tax collecting agency in your area. Many auditors also post recent sales data that can help you estimate your home's value today on the market.

To find out how much you owe on your mortgage, look at your end-of-year mortgage statements or check out this calculator from financial guru Dave Ramsey: *www.daveramsey.com/tools/mortgage-calculator*

Example: Let's say you buy a house for $200,000. You make a down payment of $20,000 and borrow $180,000. The day you buy the house, your equity is the same as the down payment ($20,000).

$200,000 (purchase price) - $180,000 (amount owed) = $20,000 (equity)

Fast-forward five years: You have been making your monthly payments and have paid down $13,000 of the mortgage debt, so you owe $167,000. During the same time, the value of the house has increased. Now it is worth $250,000. Your equity is $83,000: $250,000 (home's current appraised value) - $167,000 (amount owed) = $83,000 (equity).

House purchase price: $200,000
Amount borrowed: -$180,000
Down payment/equity: $20,000

Five years later
Amount borrowed: $180,000
Principal paid: -$13,000
Amount owed: $167,000
House's appraised value: $250,000
Amount owed: -$167,000
Equity $83,000

If you've owned your home for only a short time, you may not have much equity in your home to borrow against unless the housing prices in your area have been going up. In the housing meltdown that began in 2006, many homes dropped in value, meaning that they lost equity. If the value of your home has dropped significantly, you may even owe as much or more than your home's value, eliminating home equity loans as an option for financing your business.

Loan vs. Line of Credit

A home equity **loan** is a one-time lump sum that is paid off over a set amount of time, with a fixed interest rate and the same payments each month. Once you get the money, you cannot borrow further from the loan.

A home equity **line of credit**, or HELOC, works like a credit card – it has a revolving balance. A HELOC allows you to borrow up to a certain amount for the life of the loan – a term set by the lender. During that time, you can withdraw money as you need it. As you pay off the principal, you can use the credit again, like a credit card. A line of credit has a variable interest rate that fluctuates over the life of the loan and payments vary depending on the interest rate and the amount owed.

With either a home equity loan or HELOC, you must pay off the balance when you sell the house.

Peer-to-Peer Loans

Lending has moved online in the form of peer-to-peer loans (also known as social lending) that eliminate the middleman: the bank. These platforms allow investors to loan directly to other people through online portals such as Lending Club and Prosper.com, achieving a lower interest rate for the borrower and a higher return for the investor.

Now peer-to-peer lending sites are popping up daily, but only a few, like LendingClub.com and Prosper.com, have SEC clearance so far. Lending Club and Prosper.com allow you to borrow money from strangers – investors who want to make direct loans for a financial return. Virgin Money and LendingKarma are platforms that allow you to borrow from your friends and family, providing only the loan agreement, payment schedule, and tracking.

Most of these online peer-to-peer loans are personal loans – for debt consolidation, student loans, and other personal uses – but about 25% of the loan applications are for business purposes.

Prosper.com and LendingClub.com allow borrowers to post loan requests for up to $25,000 for up to three-year terms. Lending Club also offers a five-year term at a slightly higher interest rate. Around 95% of loan requests are funded within 14 days. In order to qualify for a peer-to-peer loan, you must have a credit score of at least 660, so check your credit first.

Advantages
- Lower interest rates than credit cards (10% vs. 14%)
- No collateral required (unsecured loans)
- Credit check is a soft inquiry instead of a hard inquiry (as with credit cards or mortgages)
- Easy applications

Disadvantages
- Less requirements and easy applications make it easy for you to make a mistake. Without a bank or investor pouring over your business plan exclaiming, "This is too expensive!" or "This is a bad risk!" who is going to ask you the tough questions? You need to be asked the tough questions.
- Shorter terms (three years) mean higher monthly payments and less flexibility if things don't work out.
- These are personal loans – not loans to the business – so ultimately, you (and your credit score) are on the hook.
- No SBA guarantee.

The application process is very simple – just your name, Social Security number, birth date, driver's license and state, and the amount you want to borrow. You'll also create a public profile with a paragraph about how you will use the loan. There's no need to go into the particulars of the brilliance of your idea – remember that these sites are public, so anyone can read your profile. Investors are mostly looking at your credit score, outstanding debt (pulled from your credit report), loan type, and amount you want to borrow – not your business plan. Your identity is kept anonymous on the site.

Not every loan gets funded. Sometimes investors are interested in high-risk, high-interest loans – other times, in low-risk, low-interest loans. These sites are relatively new – and like any new marketplace, sometimes there are more buyers than sellers or vice versa. As this book goes to print, about 10-15% of loan requests on Lending Club and Prosper.com actually get funded. The majority of borrowers are turned down for bad credit or a high debt-to-income ratio.

Every time you apply for credit or a loan, an inquiry is registered on your credit report. Having multiple inquiries in a short period of time will lower your credit score. Peer-to-peer lending sites make soft inquiries instead of hard inquiries. This means that they aren't reported to credit bureaus, so your credit score won't be affected. The loan does not show up on your credit report until after it has been funded, so you can apply for a peer-to-peer loan as many times as it takes to get one and not worry about multiple attempts lowering your credit score.

In all other ways, peer-to-peer loans are just like any loan from a bank or a credit card. Pay on time and your credit score will go up over time. Miss a payment and it will show up as a black mark on your credit report.

Lending Club and Prosper.com have fairly similar requirements and processes, but there are a few distinctions. Lending Club caters to a slightly higher credit audience. Your credit score must be over 640 with no delinquencies and you can't have a lot of existing debt. At 640, your interest rate will be over 18%. But at 780, your interest rate will be about 8%. Lending Club also has the lowest loan origination fees - 0.75-2%.

If you don't have perfect credit, check out Prosper.com. The site uses an auction system similar to eBay, so only investors are bidding on your loan. The more lenders bidding, the lower your interest rate.

	LendingClub	Prosper.com
Loan Maximums	$25,000	$25,000
Credit Qualifications:		
Minimum Credit Score	660	640
Maximum Debt-to-Income Ratio	< 25%	None
Rates & Terms:		
Borrower Interest Rates	7.9 – 19.4%	0 – 35.0%
Borrower Loan Term	3 -5 Years	3 Years
Loan Fees:		
Origination Fee (Added to Loan Amount)	0.75 – 3%	3.0%
Failed Payment Fees	$15	$15
Late Payment Fees	$15	$15
Early Payment Penalties	None	None

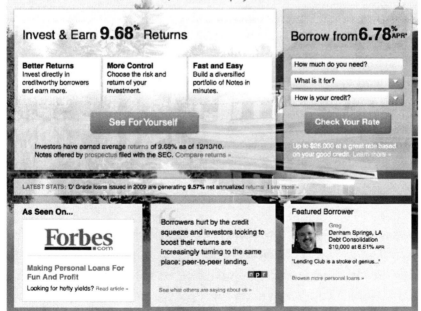

Equity

Friends and Family

Before you cast your net for angel and venture investors, look in your own backyard. In most cases, the first investors in a company are the friends or family of the entrepreneur. And as investors, they have a unique advantage: They know the entrepreneur really well.

Just as with loans from friends and family, you'll need to have a frank and honest conversation about the risks of the business, the probability of success, and the probability of failure.

No one can predict the future; we can only guess. Be sure you're making an educated guess with reality-based assumptions from reliable sources.

The best way to illustrate the probability of different outcomes is with sensitivity tables. Below is an example of a sensitivity table for a toy that sells 1,000, 10,000, or 100,000 units at varying profit margins. In the best case, the outcome is $1 million in profit. In the worst case, it's $5,000. Make sure your friends and family understand the full spectrum of risk and reward.

Margin	Number Sold		
	1,000	10,000	100,000
$5.00	$5,000	$5,000	$5,000
$7.50	$7,500	$75,000	$750,000
$10.00	$10,000	$100,000	$1,000,000

It's also very important to make sure that this is an investment they can afford to lose. If Grandpa is having a tough time making ends meet on his fixed income, he may not be able to afford to take a $10,000 loss if things don't pan out over the next few years.

Sweat Equity

If you're starting a company that is going to require a substantial amount of professional fees, such as design or software development, you might want to consider a sweat equity agreement. These arrangements eliminate the situation where you spend six months raising $50,000 in cash from investors just to hire a software developer to build a $50,000 site. Save those six months and pitch your idea to your developer to see if he'll invest his time (or "sweat") in exchange for an ownership stake in your company.

As with a normal fee-for-service contract, you want to make sure that you have a clear outline of the deliverables, scope, and price of the project. The only difference is that instead of paying in cash, the value of the contract is paid in equity (a percentage of your company).

The next question is how to value their contribution. This requires an agreement that either establishes the value of the company (similar to a pre-money valuation) or states that the first round of equity financing will establish the value of the company.

Here's how it works:

First, get a regular estimate (non-sweat equity) from your developer (or multiple developers) to get a handle on what the project will cost. Find out their hourly rate.

Next, assign an hourly rate to yourself. How many hours will you be putting into the project?

Then, build out the rest of your budget. How much will advertising, marketing, rent, and everything else cost? And who is contributing the funds for those expenses?

Here's an example:

You've spent the last month researching and designing a web application that's going to cost $10,000 and two weeks to build. Your developer agrees to work on a sweat-equity basis and you decide to personally fund the rest of the $20,000 in advertising and other expenses. You estimate that it will take you another five full months to successfully launch the app, bringing you to a total of six months of personal time invested in the project.

	Rate	Hours	Total
Developer	$100	100	$10,000
Founder	$50	1000	*$50,000*
			$60,000

Other expenses *(funded by the founder)*

Advertising	$10,000
Design	$5,000
Hosting	$4,000
Legal	$1,000
	$20,000

Equity based on cash and non-cash contributions

Developer	12.5%	$10,000
Founder	87.5%	*$70,000*
Total contributions		**$80,000**

Now double-check your work by asking yourself the following questions:

What would outside equity investors think of this valuation? Does 12.5% of the company for $10,000 sound reasonable? What does this say about the overall valuation of the company? Is the company worth $80,000 after you've worked on it for six months?

The beauty of partnering up is that you can add as many or as few team members to this structure as you want up front – as long as you accurately budget their time and contributions. As with friends and family investors or any other kind of investors, make sure that they understand the risks and probability of success or failure.

Keep an accurate accounting of all expenditures and hours worked – and make sure to handle change orders and any expansion in the scope of the project with care. If you add more hours to your developer's to-do list, that's going to cost you equity just as it would cost you cash. Similarly, if you spend more money on advertising and it comes out of your pocket, that's more equity for you. Make sure everyone that understands how the mechanics of the sweat equity agreement work – and how and when you will distribute earnings.

Raising Equity from Angel and Venture Capital Investors

Angel and venture capital investors invest (buy stock) at a certain valuation (agreed upon by owners & investors)

Pre-Money and Post-Money Valuation

	Value	Ownership
Pre-money valuation	$1,000,000	50% owners
Money raised	$1,000,000	50% investors
Post-money valuation	$2,000,000	

What does this mean? As the founder, you want a higher pre-money valuation (more ownership).

Factors that drive a higher pre-money valuation:
- No technical risk (the technology is built, tested, and working)
- Sales or sales contracts
- Intellectual property that is protected (patents, trademarks)
- High-value strategic partnerships

Most companies that raise equity require multiple rounds of investment over time. Every time you raise more money, your ownership gets further diluted. However, if you've done a good job of increasing the value of the company, you won't be diluted as much. Here's how it works:

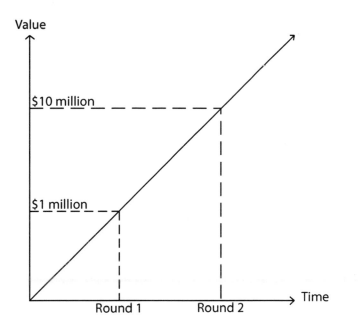

Let's say that you have a technology that will take $500,000 to prototype and test to see if it works. If it works, it will take $5 million to get it to market.

When you raise the first round of equity, all you have is an idea that is patent pending. You and your investor (Round 1 Investor) agree that your pre-revenue company is worth $1 million. They invest $500,000 in the first round. Here's what the capitalization tables look like so far:

Round 1:

	Value	Ownership
Pre-money valuation	$1,000,000	66% Founder
Money raised	$ 500,000	33% Investor
Post-money valuation	$1,500,000	

You spend the next 12 months prototyping and testing the technology – and it works! In fact, you already have customers lined up. So now, you have to raise another $5 million to get it to market. You approach another investor – let's call him Round 2 Investor. You and Round 1 Investor are both arguing for a higher valuation, while Round 2 investor argues for a lower valuation. After several serious negotiations, you, Round 1 Investor, and Round 2 Investor all agree that the value of the company is now $10 million.

Round 2:

	Value	Ownership
Pre-money valuation	$10 million	66%
		(44% Founder)
		(22% Round 1 investor)
Money raised	$ 5 million	33% Round 2 investor
Post-money valuation	$15 million	

The pre-money valuation and money raised in Round 2 result in a 66% ownership stake for all the Round 1 owners (the founder and the Round 1 investor). The Round 2 ownership stake of the Founder is calculated by multiplying the Round 1 ownership by the Round 2 ownership (66% x 66% = 44%). The Round 2 ownership stake of the Round 1 investor calculated the same way – by multiplying the Round 1 ownership by the Round 2 ownership (66% x 33% = 22%).

Raising Equity

Raising equity can be a long process – taking anywhere from six to 18 months, but you can reduce that time significantly by being prepared and by targeting multiple investors at once.

Step 1: Be prepared

Most angel investors and venture capital funds will want to see an executive summary first - a one-page document that tells them what your company does and how you make money. If the executive summary piques their interest, they'll ask for a business plan with financial projections and an investor presentation. Some will also want to see a detailed financial model. Templates for an executive summary, business plan, financial model, and investor presentation are available at the end of this chapter.

Step 2: Target multiple investors at once

Just as you might build a target list of customers, when raising capital, don't put all your eggs in one basket. By courting multiple investors at once, you'll decrease the total amount of time spent fundraising and improve your chances at getting a good deal. The chart below is an example of a target investor list.

Name	Target Amount	Probability & Status
Jim Bo	$100,000	50%, Presentation
Bob Loblaw	$50,000	25%, Business plan
Equity Partners	$250,000	50%, Presentation

Angel Investors

Angels invest about $25 billion in startups in the U.S. each year, making them the #2 source of equity investment after friends and family investors and even larger seed stage investors than venture capital funds.

Angel investors are private, high net-worth individuals who generally invest anywhere from $50,000 to $2 million in start-up companies. These investors may be organized as a formal group or operate as solo investors. Angel investors come from all industry background – and therefore invest in all kinds of industries.

These investors look for high-growth companies that can produce great returns. Because they invest at the seed stage – the riskiest stage of a company – they look for 10-30 times their investment. If they invest $50,000, they hope to get back at least $500,000 if the company does well.

Unlike venture capital funds, most angel investments are at the seed stage: in new, pre-revenue companies.

To find angel investors in your area, visit the Angel Capital Association Directory. *www.angelcapitalassociation.org/directory*

Most groups meet once a month or every other month, so contact their office well in advance to find out what their process is. Some may ask for a non-confidential version of an executive summary first; others may invite you to pitch at their next meeting.

Venture Capital Investors

Venture capital funds invest in high-growth companies that can reach at least $25 million in sales in five years – meaning big ideas and real technology. In order for a VC firm to be interested in an opportunity, there must be at least a 10% chance that they can make 30 times their money. This means that venture capital investors have to be highly selective in their investments. On average, for every hundred business plans that are evaluated by a VC fund, only one will be funded.

The venture capital industry is headquartered in Silicon Valley on Sand Hill Road in California, much like investment banking is headquartered on Wall Street in New York. Venture funds typically invest close to home, where it's easier to manage their portfolio companies, so over 50% of U.S. venture capital is invested in Silicon Valley.

Venture funds are large and professionally managed by a combination of finance professionals, industry experts, and former entrepreneurs. These funds have well-defined investment criteria and are generally organized by stage (seed, early stage, later stage) and by industry (IT, biotech, and cleantech).

Contrary to popular belief, venture funds do not primarily invest at the seed stage. In the first quarter of 2007, venture funds invested $26 million in seed-stage deals, compared with $3.1 billion in later stage deals (E&Y, Dow Jones). Still, if your company already has a track record of success and promises high returns, it's worth a shot.

Venture funds get thousands of random inquiries every year, so use your network to get an introduction. This is where having a massive LinkedIn network really helps. An introductory e-mail or call go a long way to make sure that your executive summary is at least opened. Then, make sure you have an airtight business plan, financial model, and investor presentation.

As with any outside investors, with venture capital investors, you have to be willing to give up control over major decisions. That $1 million investment isn't entirely at your disposal – and your investors will make sure of that. Angel and venture capital investors generally create a board of directors or join the existing board after an investment. The board controls all the major decisions of the company: when to raise more money, what strategy to pursue, what assets to buy or sell, who to hire, and who to fire. They have the power to fire you, to sell the company, or to fold and liquidate the company.

If you're raising venture capital and your business succeeds, be ready to sell it. Venture funds don't make their return on investment when a company "exits" – IPOs or is acquired by another company. This sale is usually seven to 10 years after the investment is made (though most business-school investor presentations show an exit after five years).

While only one in a thousand companies is venture backed, these firms are some of the fastest growing companies in our economy. Almost 20% of the companies that made the 2000 Inc 500 list, a list of the fastest growing firms in the U.S., were venture backed. And in 2000, of the more than 400 companies that went public, over half had venture backing.

In addition to growing faster than their peers, venture backed companies also fail less often. The failure rate of these companies is far below the national average. Only 10-15% of new venture-backed companies will become winners in terms of investors' expectations, but all of these firms benefit from the advice, network, and financing that these funds are able to provide.

What do Venture Capital Funds Invest in?

Venture capital funds have areas of focus that are usually well-defined. Generally, these firms are interested in technology – information technology or biotech, and more recently cleantech. This obviously leaves out most of the economy, but keep in mind that these industries were responsible for some of the largest growth in recent history and these investors are looking for growth.

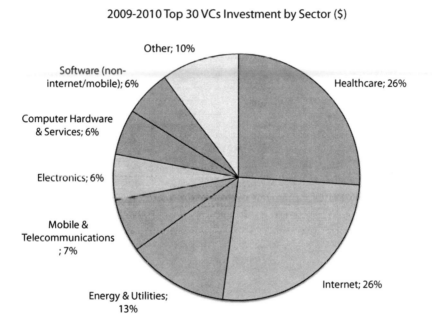

2009-2010 Top 30 VCs Investment by Sector ($)

Source: CB Insights

How to Find the Right Venture Fund for Your Business

There are very few venture capital funds that invest at the seed stage. *Entrepreneur* magazine keeps an updated list of the Top 100 Early Stage VC firms in the country.

www.entrepreneur.com/vc100/stage/early.html

Study the websites of each of these firms. You're looking for a few things:

1. Sector and industry focus: Do they only invest in biotech? This won't help you if you have a mobile game.

2. Stage and size of investment: Do they invest in pre-revenue companies? If they only invest in companies with revenues over $10 million, this is not for you.

3. Previous investments and current portfolio companies: Have they invested in similar companies or technologies (but not direct competitors)?

Characteristics of Venture-backed Companies

According to Sequoia Capital, one of the most successful VC funds in history, startups with the following characteristics have the best chance of becoming enduring companies. These are the characteristics that VCs look for in evaluating potential investments.

Clarity of Purpose. Summarize the company's business on the back of a business card.

Large Markets. Address existing markets poised for rapid growth or change. A market on the path to a $1billion potential allows for error and time for real margins to develop.

Rich Customers. Target customers who will move fast and pay a premium for a unique offering.

Focus. Customers will only buy a simple product with a singular value proposition.

Pain Killers. Pick the one thing that is of burning importance to the customer, then delight them with a compelling solution.

Think Differently. Constantly challenge conventional wisdom. Take the contrarian route. Create novel solutions. Outwit the competition.

Team DNA. A company's DNA is set in the first 90 days. All team members are the smartest or most clever in their domain. "A" level founders attract an "A" level team.

Agility. Stealth and speed will usually help beat out large companies.

Frugality. Focus spending on what's critical. Spend only on the priorities and maximize profitability.

Inferno. Start with only a little money. It forces discipline and focus. A huge market with customers yearning for a product developed by great engineers requires very little firepower.

Grants for For-Profit Entities

Business Plan Competitions & Economic Development Grants

Cities, states, universities, and other organizations many times offer small grants ($1,000-$100,000) to for-profit companies to stimulate entrepreneurship. These grants can serve as critical capital in the seed stage for concept development.

Small Business Innovation Research Program (SBIR)

The SBIR program is a congressionally mandated program for small businesses to stimulate technological innovation, increase private sector commercialization of federal R&D, and increase small business participation in federally funded R&D. Over $2 billion is awarded annually, making the SBIR program the largest source of early-stage technology financing in the US.

For-profit, high-tech companies are eligible for $150,000-$500,000 in grants through the SBIR program. Some states, such as Kentucky, have SBIR matching programs, where the state will match the federal grant, effectively increasing the grant amount to $300,000.

11 federal agencies participate in the SBIR program, including:
- Department of Agriculture
- Department of Commerce
  - NIST
  - NOAA
- Department of Defense
  - Air Force
  - Army
  - Chemical and Biological Defense Program (CBD)
  - Defense Advanced Research Projects Agency (DARPA)
  - Defense Logistics Agency (DLA)
  - Defense Microelectronics Activity (DMEA)
  - Defense Technical Information Center (DTIC)
  - Defense Threat Reduction Agency (DTRA)
  - Missile Defense Agency (formerly BMDO)
  - National Geospatial-Intelligence Agency (NGA) (formerly NIMA)
  - Navy
  - Special Operations Acquisition and Logistics Center (SOCOM)
- Department of Education
- Department of Energy
- Department of Health & Human Services (NIH, CDC, FDA, AHRQ)
  - National Cancer Institute (NCI)
- Department of Homeland Security
- Department of Transportation

- Environmental Protection Agency
- National Aeronautics & Space Administration (NASA)
- National Science Foundation

The Department of Defense and the National Institute of Health (NIH) are the largest SBIR funders.

Who Qualifies for SBIR Grants?

SBIR grants are usually awarded to university research being commercialized by a small business (less than 500 employees) that is many times partially owned by the researcher (or principal investigator). Grants are made for specific research projects that have commercial potential. The project is clearly defined and must fit within the criteria of one of the SBIR solicitations. Solicitations are made by agency, category, and subcategory.

SBIR grants can be 30-60 pages of paperwork and the proposals can take one to two months to prepare. After the application is submitted, it takes several months for the agency to review the proposal and put it through a peer review committee. It can take six months from the application deadline to find out whether a proposal will be funded.

Funds available

Phase 1 - Project feasibility - six months **up to $100k**
Phase 2 - Development to prototype - 2 years **up to $750k**
Phase 3 - Commercialization (non-SBIR funds)

SBIR Patent Rights

If a small business receives an SBIR grant, the small business retains intellectual property rights, but the government receives a royalty-free license for use of worldwide patent rights to any invention developed with the SBIR funds.

Probability of success

Depending on the agency and the competition that year, between 10-30% of SBIR applications get funded.

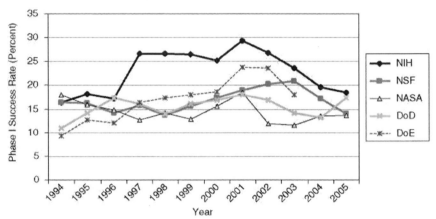

Source: National Institute of Health

Find out more information about SBIR open solicitations and how to apply at www.sbir.gov.

Grants for non-profit entities

If you're a **social entrepreneur**, you may consider filing as a non-profit. Examine your goals and business model carefully. Do you have a social mission? Does your operating model always produce a loss? If so, filing as a nonprofit may be a better pathway for you. Nonprofit status opens up the doors for federal and foundation grant funding.

Foundation Directory Online

Foundation Directory Online is a subscription website to help advance the non-profit sector through grant funding. Although it is a subscription site (starting at **$19/mo**) depending on your choice of plan), it is the leading online funding tool. Subscription is fast and easy at: http://fconline.foundationcenter.org/

Federal Grants on Grants.gov

All federal grants are posted and managed through Grants.gov, the federal government's online portal for grant funding.

Almost every federal agency posts research grant opportunities and other grant opportunities on the site. To search current postings, visit http://grants.gov.

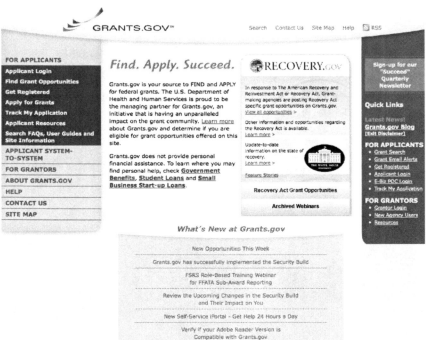

6   Create an Unforgettable Brand

"A great brand raises the bar - it adds a greater sense of purpose to the experience, whether it's the challenge to do your best in sports and fitness, or the affirmation that the cup of coffee you're drinking really matters."
– Howard Schultz, Starbucks CEO

The value of a brand

A brand is a coherent set of ideas like thoughts, feelings, perceptions, images, experiences, beliefs, and attitudes in a customer's mind. It is the personality that identifies a company and distinguishes it from others.

A brand promise is a company's vision of what its brand must be and do for the customer.

We know that customers are aware of brands when they can recall and recognize the brand under different conditions and link to the brand name, logo, jingles and other associations in their memory.

Before we dive any further into branding, let's ask ourselves what every customer asks before making a purchase: Why should I care?

Your brand is your company's largest and **most important asset.** When we look at the balance sheet of a publicly traded company like Coca-Cola, a brand is listed as an intangible asset, as opposed to tangible assets such as buildings, equipment, computers and all the other assets that we can see, touch, and price easily in a market.

The value of these brands – these intangible assets – can be huge. Analysts value Coca-Cola's brand at almost $70 billion*. The enterprise value alone of Coca-Cola is about $140 billion, meaning that **Coca-Cola's brand is 50% of the company's value.**

---

* While on the balance sheet Goodwill and Intangible Assets only account for about $13 billion of the company's current assets, it's important to note that the $70 billion is what analysts think the brand is actually worth – its market value. (Source: USA Today)

Brands are often understated on the balance sheet, but their value is priced clearly when a company is sold. For instance, when Philip Morris bought Kraft, they paid nearly six times the value of the company because the value of the Kraft brand was vastly understated on the balance sheet.

80 percent of purchasing is emotional

People are mostly emotional – not rational – beings. Your brand is the emotional heart of your company. According to Kevin Roberts of Saatchi & Saatchi, emotion, intuition, long-term memories and unconscious motivations make up as much as 80 percent of our decision-making processes. This leaves just 20 percent to logic.

What does this mean for marketers? You may offer the best deal, but if people really identify with your competitor's brand, you're in serious danger of losing the sale.

Perhaps nowhere else is branding's emotional influence on purchasing as apparent as in the breakfast cereal aisle. Look at Kellogg's Frosted Flakes, for instance. Generic frosted corn flakes cost 50 percent less, but taste similar and may even be made in the same factory. Yet most people buy the branded flakes. This is the power of the brand. Brands establish preferences, loyalty, and command price premiums. And the most powerful brands tap into emotions.

First impressions are lasting impressions

Many startups begin selling their product or service first, "branding" as they go – creating logos, letterhead, ads, and sales brochures on an as-needed basis. Just as with job interviews and first dates, you want to make sure that your brand puts its best foot forward because you may not get another chance. Think of your brand name as your nametag, your tagline as your handshake, and your logo and other designs as your outfit. This is your livelihood, so dress up!

Your brand should be planned and articulated as carefully as your business plan or resume – and well in advance of launching your product. A name change, logo change, and other changes down the road will confuse your customers and leave them with one sure impression: that your brand is inconsistent.

Branding Project Plan

This chapter is a step-by-step tactical plan for creating a new brand from scratch.

1. **Research** – 8-12 hours *(on your own)*
   a. Customers
   b. Competitors
   c. Unmet Needs
   d. Brand Comparison
   e. Customer-focused Value Proposition
2. **Brainstorm** – 4-8 hours *(with 5 friends)*
   a. Present research findings (30 mins)
   b. Create Brand Identity (Personality) in 3 exercises (1-2 hours)
        i. Icebreaker
       ii. Adjectives
      iii. Values
   c. Name options (1-2 hours)
   d. Tagline options (30 mins)
   e. Touch point ideas (1 hour)
   f. Get feedback on names, taglines, and touch points from several outsiders
3. Create a **Design Brief** *(on your own):* Synthesize your customer research, competitor research, value proposition, brand identity, name, tagline, and touch points for your designer
4. Hire **Designer** *(on your own)*
   a. Logo
   b. Fonts & colors
   c. Touch points
5. **Get feedback** on logo & touch points *(with 5 friends)*
6. **Execution** & **Delivery** *(on your own)*
   a. Create message
   b. Create touch points
7. **Be consistent** with your brand

Customer Research

Customers can be businesses or individuals. The *decision maker* or *customer* – the person who buys – is usually the *end user* as well – the person who uses the product or service. For example, when you buy shampoo and conditioner for yourself, you are both the decision maker and the end user and you are both buying and consuming the product. In other words, you are a *consumer*.

But in some cases the decision maker is not the user. For example, if you are selling children's vitamins, you'll have to direct much of your marketing towards parents because the parent is the decision maker. Yet, you still must have the child's wants and needs in mind since the child is the end user.

B2B marketing, or marketing to businesses, and *B2C marketing*, or marketing to consumers, are vastly different animals, but both require intimate knowledge of the customer, whether that customer is a business or a consumer.

B2B Market Research

Marketing to businesses is more of a science and less of an art. Businesses are profit-driven and less emotional than consumers, so marketing efforts are focused on demonstrating some strategic, operational, or functional benefit to the organization.

Broadly, these marketing messages communicate to businesses that your offering either:
  1. Increases revenues for their company in some way
  2. Decreases costs for their company in some way

Businesses may include such organizations as manufacturers, service providers, resellers, governments, and nonprofits. These firms evaluate offerings in more detail than the typical consumer, and the decision process usually involves more than one person.

First, you'll need to describe what **need** your offering satisfies – whether it's strategic, operational, or functional. Then, you'll need to identify who the primary decision maker is and who the end users are for your offering.

Strategic offerings are in some way important to the enterprise mission, objectives and operational oversight. For example, a service that helps raise equity capital would be considered a strategic service. The primary decision maker for strategic buys is usually the top-level executive management.

Operations offerings affect the general operating policies and procedures of the company. Examples might include an employee insurance plan or a corporate e-mail system. The primary decision maker for operational buys is usually the operations manager for that department.

Functional offerings deal with a specific function within the company such as accounts payable, cleaning and maintenance, human resources, marketing, inventory control, etc. This is the most likely domain for a product or a service. The primary decision maker for functional offerings is usually the manager of that specific department, but others may also get involved if it's a large purchase.

Many different types of **profile** variables can be applied to business buyers as a way to segment the market. The three most common are geography, type of company, and behavioral characteristics.

Geographic segmentation simply refers to where the business is located. Your target market may be defined by contract as a certain territory – or shipping costs and distance from the vendor may be a critical factor in serving customers.

Business customers can also be segmented according to the **type of company**, for instance:
- Company size
- Industry
- Decision-making unit
- Purchase Criteria

Behavioral characteristics like patterns of purchasing behavior can also be a basis for segmentation. Such behavioral characteristics may include:
- Usage rate
- Buying status: potential, first time, regular, etc.
- Purchase procedure: sealed bids, negotiations, etc.

Build a Target Customer List

Whether you're making a strategic, operations, or functional sale, you'll want to start by crafting a target customer list, detailing the primary decision maker and the end users and other stakeholders. This list will help you stay on top of revenue goals – and help focus your research efforts.

Target Customer	Primary Decision Maker	End User & Stakeholders	Target Revenue	Probability
ACE Hardware	Store Manager	Consumer, Salespeople	$100,000	20%
Hallmark Stores	District Store Manager	Consumer, Salespeople	$500,000	30%
Yankee Candle	Corporate Buyer	Consumer, Salespeople	$400,000	20%

Market Data Sources for Businesses

Next, you'll want to compile relevant data on those target companies and find similar companies that could be potential customers.

If your customers are publicly traded companies, you're in luck. There's a wealth of free information available in their annual reports about their operations, strategies, and financial performance. Market research firms and other industry analysts also publish reports on specific companies and industries. These reports can be purchased and downloaded for around $100 typically, but can range in price from $10-$10,000.

Top resources for business market research

Resource & Website	Description
EDGAR Online www.sec.gov/edgar.shtml	Annual Reports (10k Filings) and other financial reports on publicly traded companies
Hoovers www.hoovers.com	Find competitors, revenues, and executive summaries of public and private companies
U.S. Census Bureau www.census.gov	Search for industry information by SIC or NAICS classification

Consumer Market Research

Before marketing any product or service to consumers, it's important to understand who they are and what they need. This is where consumer research comes in.

First, you'll want to identify the scope of your target market. Is your product for the masses, like razor blades and paper towels? Or does your product have a narrower, more defined target market, like a Corvette? In most cases, you will address more than one segment of the market (for instance, convenience-seeking suburban moms and health-conscious single professionals). Regardless of how big your market is, the more you can define your target-market segments, the more useful your consumer-market research will be.

In order to segment your market well, we need to identify the variables that split the market into actionable segments. There are two types of market-research variables:
1. Needs
2. Profilers

Profilers are the descriptive, measurable customer characteristics (such as location, age, nationality, gender, income) that can be used to inform a segmentation exercise.
There are four major types of consumer profile segmentation: *geographic, demographic, psychographic, and behavioral.*

Geographic segmentation is defined as subdividing markets into segments based on location, the regions, countries, cities and towns where people live and work. The following are some examples of geographic variables often used in segmentation:
  • Region: by continent, country, state, or even neighborhood

- Size of metropolitan area: segmented according to size of city
- Population density: often classified as urban, suburban, or rural
- Climate: according to weather patterns common to certain geographic regions

The best free resource for geographic segmentation in the U.S. is the U.S. Census Bureau, *www.census.gov*.

Demographic segmentation is the most common type of consumer market segmentation. Demographics are frequently used because they are often strongly related to demand and relatively easy to measure. The most popular characteristics for demographic segmentation are age, gender, family, life cycle, income and education. Common demographic segmentation variables include:
- Age, gender, marital status, children, family size
- Income, occupation, education
- Religion, race, nationality, culture

Many of these variables have standard categories for their values. For example, family life cycle often is expressed as bachelor, married with no children (DINKS: Double Income, No Kids), full-nest, empty-nest, or solitary survivor. Some of these categories have several stages, for example, full-nest I, II, or III, depending on the age of the children.

The best free resource for demographic segmentation in the U.S. is the U.S. Census Bureau, *www.census.gov*.

Psychographic segmentation divides buyers into different groups based on social class, lifestyle or personality characteristics. People in the same demographic group can have different psychographic makeup. So psychographic segmentation helps the marketer in examining attributes related to how a person thinks, feels, and behaves. Activities, interests, and opinions (AIO) surveys are one tool for measuring lifestyle.

- Social class
- Lifestyle type
- Personality type/traits
- Activities, Interests
- Opinions, Attitudes, Values

Behavioral segmentation divides buyers into groups based on product-related behavior such as their knowledge, attitudes, uses or responses to a product.

- Product usage: light, medium, heavy users
- Brand loyalty: none, medium, high
- Type of user: e.g., recreational, special occasions
- Buying patterns: e.g., stockpile, routine
- Occasions: holidays and events that stimulate purchases
- User status: potential, first time, regular, etc.
- Readiness to buy
- Benefits sought

Needs-based Segmentation

Needs are an essential variable of consumer research and differ from profilers in that they are product and feature-specific. The four main types of customer needs are:

1. **Functionality** (Can it do more?) Do a comparison of features. Does their utility pocket knife offer tweezers? Scissors? A screwdriver?

2. **Reliability** (Is it more reliable?) Look for any relevant information concerning breakdown, replacement, etc.

3. **Convenience** (Is it more convenient?) Do they offer a mobile app? A drive-thru? A travel size? Check into all the convenience factors.

4. **Price** (Is it cheaper?) By how much? Look into the relative prices – high and low – as well as the alternatives. How would an economist or Vulcan view this product or service?

Needs-based segmentation can be helpful not only in identifying consumer segments, but also in defining the competition.

First, let's look at the competitive landscape and boil down your competitor's offering and your offering on those four dimensions. **Score your offering and each of your competitors,** rating them 1-4 on a scale. Are they missing something?

		Low			High
1.	**Functionality**	1	2	3	4
2.	**Reliability**	1	2	3	4
3.	**Convenience**	1	2	3	4
4.	**Price**	1	2	3	4

If you have more than one competitor, it may be helpful to sketch them out on a graph. The graph below shows the difference between two offerings – one for a feature-seeker and one for a price-shopper.

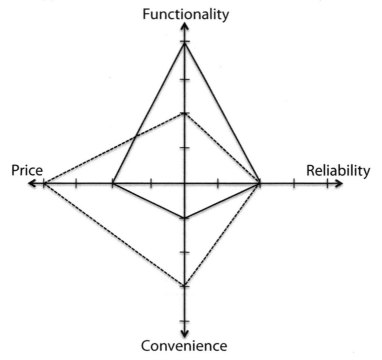

Competitor Research: Catalog the competition

Regardless of whether you have a product or a service, before you start thinking of names, logos, and advertising campaigns, look to see what's out there. Who is "on the shelf" or "in the Yellow Pages" next to you?

Where do you compete? In the retail store? Online? You're in a battle for customers, so make sure that you know which field(s) of battle matters most.

For example, if you're launching a product, you'll want to walk the aisles of the retail stores that sell those products, check out the competition, talk to the salespeople, and check out the price points. You need as much data and examples as possible. If possible, buy each competitive item and examine it closely.

- What's the quality of the packaging? What materials are used?
- What's the price point?
- What does the sales person or store manager think about the item? How could it be better? What do customers say?

Brand Positioning

Your brand will ultimately determine your sales and market share relative to your competitors. Now that you've created a thorough picture of the current market, think about how your brand would fit into that market. Brand positioning defines brand strategy, creative direction, messaging, and tone.

Brand Comparison Exercise

Take all of the advertisements, product samples, media articles, and competitor research that you've compiled and create a brand comparison chart that lists all of your competitors and each of the following:

1. Competitors' **value proposition**
What features do they offer? What promises and claims do they make? What's their tagline? Use the needs segmentation you did in the previous section to compare the value proposition in terms of functionality, reliability, convenience, and price – as well as specific features that may exist (e.g., longer shelf life and fewer calories, or softer fabric and custom monogramming, or free shipping and no-hassle refunds)

2. Competitors' **touch points**
How do they deliver their message? Do they send direct mail or e-mail? Sign up for their mailing list. If they have ads online, in print, or elsewhere, start to keep a running scrapbook of their ads.

3. Competitors' **brand awareness**
Have people even heard of this brand? Do they ask for the product/service by brand name? How long have they been in business? How many customers do they have and how long have they had them?

4. Competitors' **brand identity**

What adjectives come to mind for each of your competitors? What words do they use to describe themselves? What do customers think of the brand? What elements does the name have?

Catalog the following Brand Attributes for each of your competitors:

    a) Brand Name
    b) Tagline
    c) Brand Adjectives – adjectives used to describe the brand by customers, media, etc.
    d) Brand Promise (if published)
    e) Brand Values (if published) and
    f) Brand Colors and Fonts
    g) Brand Icons (like the Lion of Merrill Lynch)

Example Brand Identity Comparison

Name & Logo	NIVEA	L'ORÉAL
Tagline	"All that skin needs to live"	"Because you're worth it"
Brand Values and Adjectives	Dermatological	French
	Clinical	Style
	Based in science	Fashion
	Trust	Premium
	Reliability	Elegance
	Accessibility	Cutting-edge
	High end, available for the masses	Beauty
		Cosmetic
Colors	Blue & White	Black & Gold

The myth of "no competition"

Many strategy books have been written about "white space" or "blue oceans" – a kind of business Utopia where no competition exists. Well, white space comes with its own set of headaches.

Sometimes, the reason that no competition exists is simply that no opportunity exists.

Even when you are the first to market, you are still competing against a phantom: non-consumption. Just because there's no competition doesn't mean there's no alternative. The alternative is not buying your product altogether.

White space is inherently riskier. No one has demonstrated feasibility yet – be it technical, business model, or otherwise. In many cases, being a second or third mover – a "fast follower" – is an advantage. Facebook was a fast follower to Friendster and MySpace. Pepsi entered the market after Coke.

Also, keep in mind that if you are the first mover and you're successful, you too will have competition someday.

While you may truly have no competition today that will serve as a starting point for positioning your brand, you still have research to do before you can get started. First, you want to go back to your customers and benchmark the "current state." Find out what feelings and messages exist as alternatives.

For example, before there were cars, Henry Ford still had competition that was literally alive and well: the horse. Ford had to position cars as not just an odd bit of technology or a toy, but as a viable transportation alternative to the horse.

Create a Customer-Focused Value Proposition

Innovation guru Doug Hall explains how to create a customer-focused value proposition in his book "Jumpstart Your Business Brain." The book explains how to increase your product's chances of success by translating features into **overt benefits**, explaining your product's **dramatic difference**, and giving your customer a **reason to believe** your claims.

Now is the time to stop talking like an inventor and start talking like a salesman. Inventors are in love with the features of their product – but we need to articulate these features as customer benefits and make it exceedingly obvious why a customer should buy your product instead of something else. Customers are smart, but they're busy, so we need to speak their language. Cut the jargon, delete the acronyms, and start talking benefits!

Using the demographic and psychographic research you've conducted on your customers, try to put yourself in their shoes and approach your own product or service as if you'd never seen it before. Ask yourself, "What results will that feature bring me?"

Why should the customer care? Customers are inundated with thousands of messages every day, so don't assume that yours is special. Make your message stand out at a glance. "Hey! This orange juice builds strong bones!" "Hey! This car is safer in a crash!"

It's time to focus. While your product or service may have 50 features, **pick the three to five most important and most unique features of your product**. Overtly tell customers why your offering is different: why it's is the best, the first, the only … versus what's available. Do you have a numeric promise like "lasts three times longer" or "uses 50% of the energy"?   Be as specific about the benefits as possible.

You only have five seconds for them to read one simple sentence about your offering! That's it! Then they'll either buy or they won't. Only 1% of your customers are going to read your whole brochure or your whole website or your whole package! The other 99% are going to look at the name, the benefits, the price, and make a decision. If they decide not to buy, they won't come back to look again. So forget the clutter: What's your big WOW?

Steps:

1. List all the features of your product and pick the three to five most important and unique.

2. Now, translate those three to five features into customer benefits – the results the customer will experience. Don't use any technical terms.   Be as clear, simple, and obvious as possible, using language a 12-year-old can understand. Write directly to the final decision maker about each feature, starting with "the benefit to you is…" and not "the customer will get…"

Example: Tropicana Orange Juice

Features:	Benefits:
Vacuum-sealed container	→ Stays fresh longer
Not from concentrate	→ Tastes great
Contains calcium	→ Builds strong bones

Example: Jeep Grand Cherokee

Features:	Benefits:
Stabilization control	→ Reduces rollover risk
Rearview camera	→ Helps you backup and park safely
Variable Valve Timing	→ Go 500 miles on one tank of gas
Side & rear airbags	→ Reduces backseat passenger injury

3. Align your benefits with the final decision maker. Who is going to buy your product or service? Make sure that your benefits and results are clearly communicated to that specific decision maker. Your answers may give you even more insight into your target customer.

Example: Tropicana Orange Juice
Benefits: Decision Maker:
Builds strong bones →   Parents with young kids
                              Older women with bone loss

4. Provide real reasons to believe. Why should a customer believe you – a new brand? What proof or credibility do you have? Here are 6 ways (in order of effectiveness) to prove your point:

   1. Tell The Truth
      o   Simply do these steps…
      o   We can deliver because…
   2. Testimonials
      o   Experts say…
      o   Past clients say…
   3. Data/Test Results
      o   The data indicates…
      o   In a side-by-side test…
   4. Demonstration
      o   Try it yourself…
      o   For a sample…
   5. Guarantee
      o   We'll guarantee you…
      o   100% money back if…
   6. Pedigree
      o   Professional Titles/Awards
      o   It was developed by…

How to Brainstorm

Now that you've finished your research, you're going to need the help of five creative friends to come up with a name, tagline, brand identity, and touch points that make sense.

Materials needed:
5 creative friends (groups of 5-6 are the best size for these brainstorming exercises)
1 case of beer or other age-appropriate beverage
Props – ads, packaging, etc – from your competitors
Pictures of your target customer
Computer with Internet access
Thesaurus or dictionary
Post-it notes
Dot stickers
Whiteboard
Markers

Process:
1.   Brainstorm for quantity, coming up with as many ideas as you can.
2.   Discuss the pros and cons of some of the best ideas.
3.   Narrow the list by either
     a. Process of elimination
     b. Power dot voting. If you want to narrow the list to five concepts, give each person five sticker dots. Post all the ideas on the wall and have everyone vote all at once by placing dots on their favorite ideas. They can place all their dots on their favorite idea or spread their dots (votes) across multiple ideas.

Rules:
1.   Keep the exercise positive and fun.
2.   There are no dumb ideas – write it down, move on, and come back to it later.

Are you ready? Because in this brainstorming session, we're going to come up with your brand identity (personality), name, tagline, and delivery touch points.

Creating a Brand Personality

The building blocks of a brand's personality are adjectives - usually adjectives that we would use to describe people, such as glamorous, trustworthy, hip, or professional. For example, Marlboro is a "masculine" brand, while Virginia Slims are "feminine." Nike is innovative and athletic. Apple is young, stylish, cool, and casual.

People personify things on a routine basis. We personify pets, cars and boats all the time. We assign human-like attributes to essentially anything with a name — people, places, things, and yes, even products and companies. We rely most often on the one analogy we understand best: what it means to be human.

Your brand as a real person in a relationship

Imagine your brand is a real person. Are they a man or a woman? Are they young or old? How are they dressed?

Now imagine that your brand is a real person who has a real relationship with your customer. What is their relationship like? Are they friends? Is your brand a mentor or an adviser to your customer? If your brand is an adviser to your customer, a "punk" brand personality is probably the wrong tone. Use this visual exercise to start thinking of the personality you want to create for your brand.

Carl Jung's Archetypal Theory

Archetypes are the original model or mold for characters that are repeated constantly in different myths stories. They have similar personalities and traits – the hero, the adventurer, the lover, the outlaw, and the sage. Psychologist Carl Jung created a theory about archetypes in the early 20th century. He wrote, "There are forms or images of a collective nature which … are imprinted and hardwired into our psyches."

We intuitively "get" archetypes because we've seen them over and over in our favorite movies and stories. In branding, these archetypes allow us to take shortcuts in creating brands that people can easily identify with and understand.

Archetypal Branding was developed by Carol Pearson and is explained in her book, "The Hero and The Outlaw: Building Extraordinary Brands Through the Power of Archetypes." The system consists of two dimensions: self-focused versus group-oriented, and order versus change.

Apple and Harley Davidson's brands are excellent examples of the Rebel archetype. FedEx and Wheaties are examples of the Hero archetype. Campbell's Soup and AllState Insurance are Caregiver brands. REI and Jeep are Explorer brands. Victoria's Secret and Calvin Klein are both excellent examples of the Lover archetype. For a quick tutorial and more examples of the archetype branding system, visit *www.herowithin.com/hero.htm*. Explore these different personality types to spark some ideas about your brand's personality.

Brainstorming

Icebreaker

For these exercises, it's really important that the group has fun and stays positive while remaining thoughtful, insightful, and relevant. Get the ideas flowing and the group talking by starting out with these four fun branding analogies: the car, the celebrity, the animal, and ideal spokesperson.

If your brand were a **car**, what kind of car would it be? Why? Be specific: make, model, and color. Is it a coupe or sedan? Import or domestic? Convertible? Are you the safe choice, like Volvo? Or are you flashy, like a Ferrari?

If your brand was a famous **celebrity**, who would it be and why? What traits do they possess that are shared with your brand?

If your brand were an **animal**, what kind of animal would it be? Are you exotic like a zebra? If you're going to choose a dog, at least get specific and clarify the breed. Are you a golden retriever or a bulldog – and why?

If your organization could choose anyone in the world as its **spokesperson**, who would it be and why? Would you pick someone from your local community or a respected actor – or a fictional character like the GEICO gecko?

Branding Icebreaker Example

	Car	Celebrity	Animal	Spokesperson
Abby	Jeep	John Wayne	Cheetah	Jeff Probst
Carlo	Hummer	Indiana Jones	Lion	Harrison Ford
Sarah	SUV	John Wayne	Yellow Lab	Lance Armstrong
Mick	Jeep	John Wayne	Dog	Lance Armstrong

Brand Adjectives

Spend an hour or two brainstorming a set of adjectives with your five friends that describe your brand. First, think of _at least 50_ — and then narrow the list to _three to five most important_.

- Masculine or feminine
- Simple or complex
- Young or old
- Breakthrough or established
- Individualist or group-oriented
- Soft or hard
- Dark or light
- Warm or cool
- Fast or slow
- Conventional or eccentric
- Exclusive or accessible
- Eastern or Western
- Casual or formal
- Local or global
- Gray or colorful
- Subtle or bright
- Necessity or luxury
- Expensive or economical
- Playful or serious
- Modern or classic
- Raw or refined
- Exotic or commonplace
- Sporty or elegant
- Adventurous or secure
- Conservative or progressive
- Urban or outdoorsy
- Playful or serious

- Big or small
- Leader or underdog
- Stylish or practical
- Outspoken or reserved
- Dynamic or stable
- Predictable or surprising

Other brand personality adjectives:

Inclusive	Ambitious
Honest	Cosmopolitan
Persuasive	Healthy
Clear	Traditional
Humorous	Broad
Intelligent	Funky
Encouraging	Mature
Welcoming	Universal
Confident	Detailed
Direct	Spiritual
Open	Robotic
Optimistic	Graceful
Friendly	Flexible
Caring	Relaxed
Courageous	Independent
Trustworthy	Innovative
Inspirational	Experienced
Dynamic	Rational
Determined	Factual
Professional	Academic
Passionate	Green
Reliable	Functional

Brand Values

Now think of your most important brand values. What does your brand believe in? Is your brand feminine and classic, but believe in health and the environment? Below are a few examples of brand values:

Community	Education
Nurturing	Pragmatism
Innovation	Openness
Value	People
Diversity	Precision
Reliability	Safety
Trust	Affordability
Optimism	Integrity
Irreverence	Knowledge
Teamwork	Quality
Family	Cleanliness
Competition	Fairness
Entertainment	Security
Connection	Honesty
Authenticity	High-tech
Commitment	Growth
Disclosure	Customer focus
Fun	Creativity
Performance	Democracy
Simplicity	Environment
Comfort	Responsiveness
Health	Golden Rule

Make a Brand Promise

A brand promise is a vision of what the brand must be and do for the consumer. Starbucks' brand promise is to "provide the highest quality coffee, exceptional customer service, and a truly uplifting Starbucks Experience." FedEx stands for "peace of mind."

Before you do much promoting, you should ensure that you are delivering on the promise – whether it's low price, high quality, reliability, or accessibility - and do it consistently. It's that level of consistency that builds loyalty and respect among customers, leading to revenue growth.

Below are some common brand promises:
1. Product leadership (having the best products in the marketplace) like Herman Miller or Apple
2. Operational excellence like FedEx
3. Lower prices like Wal-Mart's "everyday low prices" or Southwest Airlines' "low fares"
4. Great customer service like Zappos.com and Nordstrom

Once you have a good idea of your brand's position relative to your competitors and the values of your brand, take a stab at writing a promise to your customers. This is the promise that you'll want to keep consistent in your messaging and in the delivery of your product or service, no matter what.

Under promise and over deliver. When writing your brand promise, try to stick to one promise initially - and definitely not more than two. Three promises are downright unrealistic – and there's nothing worse for a brand than breaking a brand promise.

Create a Brand Name

Your brand name should accomplish two things:

1. **Explain your business to potential customers.** You can never be too obvious. Regardless of the type of name you select, make sure your customers can recognize what services the business provides, based on the name of the company (example: Friendly Dog Walkers or Bright Accounting).

2. **Differentiate your business from your competitors.** ABC Accounting and AAA Accounting are so close that even longtime customers may confuse them. Your brand name is your first opportunity to explain how you are different, so as you look at your brand-positioning charts, if price is your primary differentiator, consider using words that describe that point of differentiation – words like discount, affordable, econo-, and savings.

There are several **types of brand names**:

Descriptive names describe a product benefit or function like Gentle Dental, Whole Foods or Snappy Maid Service. The primary benefit of choosing a descriptive name is that potential customers know exactly what you're selling. The downside of descriptive names is that these names are drawn from a small pool of relevant keywords, so if you have several competitors, it will be hard to find a name that isn't taken – or a name that's distinct enough. Domain names will also be a little harder to find. If you're too descriptive and not distinctive enough, it might prevent you from getting a trademark.

Alliteration and **names that rhyme** stick in the mind like Reese's Pieces or Dunkin' Donuts or Stanley Steemer. Alliteration and rhymes are fun to say, meaning that they lend themselves easily to viral and word-of-mouth marketing. They are also easier to remember. Names that are both descriptive and either rhyme or have alliteration are dynamite combinations: They tell the customer in very clear language what the product or service does and they're memorable. -For instance, Gentle Dental is both descriptive (the dentists are gentle) and it rhymes, making it easier to remember.

Experiential and evocative names are rare, engaging, and powerful differentiators. These names evoke a relevant vivid image - like "Amazon" or "Crest." This direct connection to something real helps make these names more memorable. When the image or experience is relevant to the product or service, they can be even better than descriptive names. For example, web browsers such as Explorer, Navigator, and Safari, call to mind the feeling of discovery, which is a relevant experience for an Internet browser. Experiential names are great for products and services that are first to market, but over-usage makes them less distinctive, and therefore less effective, in the long run. For instance, Explorer, Navigator, and Safari are also the names of SUVs. When an experiential or evocative name is too abstracted and not directly connected to the product or service, this can create confusion. If the name is too out of synch with the brand positioning, it's an ugly mess.

Made-up/Invented names, like Wii or Kodak, are unique, making them easier to trademark, but in some cases, harder to remember unless they're experiential like "Snapple". Made-up or invented names that don't have a relevant or clear connection to the product or service are generally harder to remember, meaning that you'll have to spend more on marketing in order to make a clear impression. However, the name Wii sounds like "Weee!" – a shout of joy on a rollercoaster, calling to mind motion and fun. This is an appropriate name for a video game system that requires real movement and interaction from the user.

Foreign words, especially those adopted from romance languages such as Latin, Spanish, and French, sound familiar, but are still unique, making them easier to trademark. If you use a foreign word in your brand name, make sure that the word is easy to spell (otherwise your customers will have a hard time finding you online) and easy to say (otherwise you'll undermine your own natural word-of-mouth marketing). Online translators such as AltaVista's Babelfish can be helpful – as are Latin and Greek root words.

Geographic names can help call to mind powerful images of mountains, oceans, and other landscapes – or define the market you serve. Many brands are named for regions and landmarks like Fuji Film or Patagonia brand clothing. If you're serving a local market, a geographically relevant name will actually help you with Search Engine Optimization (SEO). For instance, if you have a plumbing company that serves the City of Norwood, Norwood Plumbing is a great name. Customers searching for plumbers in your area will find you more easily online that Johnson & Sons Plumbing in Norwood.

Initials or Acronyms such as UPS (United Parcel Service) or IBM (International Business Machines) are common types of names, but generally evolve naturally as a result of long names of established companies that are shortened for convenience. Initials are easy to forget if they are on their own (AAA vs. AAA Driving School), meaning that you'll spend more money on marketing before you can make a lasting impression. Initials also offer little differentiation from competitors (ABC Dental vs. Gentle Dental, or AAA Driving School vs. Safety First Driving School).

Companies named after people, usually the founders like Hewlett-Packard or Disney, are common especially in professional service firms, such as law firms and accounting firms. Some brand names come from fictional characters, like Nike (a mythological character), or Betty Crocker, a housewife invented by ad executives.

Brainstorm for Quantity – 100 names

Once you understand what you want your company name to convey, it's time to brainstorm some names with your five brainstorming buddies.

Use the **list of values and adjectives** you just created and leverage resources like **a dictionary or thesaurus**. Keep the room comfortable, keep the caffeine or adult beverages flowing, and keep the atmosphere positive and fun.

In this short time, the goal is to come up with as many names as possible – thinking of different combinations, root words, and angles. Remember the rules: There are no bad ideas! We're looking for quantity now, not quality. Try to come up with **at least 100 names**.

Think about
- Words that describe your industry or the products or services you offer
- Words that describe the benefits of using your products or services
- Words that describe your competitors and the differences between your products and services and those of your competitors
- Words and phrases that evoke the feelings you want your customers to feel when they see your brand name

Select the Quality – the top 5 names

Now narrow the list down to five names by evaluating them with the following criteria:

1. Short
2. Simple
3. Relevant
4. Easy to spell
5. Easy to remember

Names that are fun to say (like Reese's Pieces) or evoke a positive and memorable image (like Amazon) get extra credit since sound and sight help make those names more memorable.

Examples of some great names

TotalGym - Exercise Equipment
Smoothie King – Smoothies
Stanley Steemer – Steam Cleaning Service

Things to avoid:

1. Fads and Trends – In the early '90s everything was E-something. In the early 2000s everything was I-something. Try to avoid the latest fad and pick something timeless.
2. Intentional misspellings – Misspellings make it hard for customers to find you on the web or in the phone book.
3. Bad acronyms – Acronyms are hard to remember (and it's even harder to remember what they stand for!). Make sure to check for unfortunate acronyms like "Apple Support Services" (ASS).
4. Too narrow – Naming your business "Toledo Antique Watches" is too narrow in two ways. First, what if you want to sell antique pens as well? Or new watches? And what if

you expand to Columbus or Cleveland? Make sure your name doesn't limit the scope or geography of your business.

5. Plain words – Plain words make it very difficult to stand out from the crowd.

6. Obscure words – Obscure business names are often difficult to spell and even more difficult to remember. These words can be tempting choices because they're unique, but make sure they're relevant. You don't want to spend your entire marketing budget explaining how your name is relevant to your business; it should be obvious.

Check Trademark and Domain Name Availability

Once you've created an exhaustive list of names, start checking domain name availability and trademarks. Domain names may be taken – or may be for sale.

Trademarks

Go to USPTO.gov to the trademark search tool, TESS. Search for live and dead trademarks in your field by entering each name into the TESS search tool. Trademarks are domain specific in most cases. For instance, Coca-Cola is a beverage trademark. If you wanted to brand a car Coca-Cola, you may be able to do so (though it wouldn't make much sense).

United States Patent and Trademark Office

Home Site Index Search FAQ Glossary Guides Contacts eBusiness eBiz alerts News Help

Trademarks > Trademark Electronic Search System (TESS)

TESS was last updated on Fri Nov 12 04:05:47 EST 2010

TESS Home NEW USER STRUCTURED FREE FORM BROWSE DICT SEARCH OG BOTTOM HELP PREV LIST CURR LIST NEXT LIST FIRST DOC PREV DOC NEXT DOC LAST DOC

Logout Please logout when you are done to release system resources allocated for you.

Start List At: on Jump to record: **Record 32 out of 175**

TARR Status ASSIGN STATUS TDR TTAB Status (Use the "Back" button of the Internet Browser to return to TESS)

Word Mark	COCA-COLA
Goods and Services	IC 032. US 045 046 048. G & S: Non-alcoholic beverages, namely, soft drinks; and syrups and concentrates for making beverages, namely, soft drinks. FIRST USE: 20021215. FIRST USE IN COMMERCE: 20030101
Mark Drawing Code	(3) DESIGN PLUS WORDS, LETTERS, AND/OR NUMBERS
Design Search Code	26.11.21 - Rectangles that are completely or partially shaded 26.17.02 - Bands, wavy; Bars, wavy; Lines, wavy; Wavy line(s), band(s) or bar(s)
Serial Number	78509545
Filing Date	November 1, 2004
Current Filing Basis	1A
Original Filing Basis	1A
Published for Opposition	April 3, 2007
Registration Number	3252896
Registration Date	June 19, 2007
Owner	(REGISTRANT) The Coca-Cola Company CORPORATION DELAWARE One Coca-Cola Plaza Atlanta GEORGIA 30313
Attorney of Record	Bruce W. Baber
Prior Registrations	0022406;1057885;2992985;AND OTHERS
Description of Mark	The stippling in the drawing is not intended to indicate color.
Type of Mark	TRADEMARK
Register	PRINCIPAL

If the trademark is available, double-check to make sure that the name meets the trademark criteria (see Trademarks in Chapter 10). Steer clear of names that are similar to your competitors – you don't want to get sued for trademark or copyright infringement.

Domain Names

If the domain is owned, but is not in use, it is probably for sale. The question is: how much? Many domain-name holding companies start out at a **minimum of $5,000** asking price. Many of these companies are foreign and the negotiations are reminiscent of a used car lot or a bazaar, so be professional and get into the spirit of it! Keep in mind that you may be their only interested buyer in months – or ever – so start negotiating. You have hundreds of other name options, so feel free to walk away – they may come back with a better offer. If not, you will likely have an opportunity to change your mind. If you're lucky, you'll be able to talk them down to $500 or $1,000 if the name is not in demand.

There are also some processes in place where business owners can go to ICANN and file a complaint based on the fact that their trademarked domain name is being held for ransom. Some businesses have gone through this process successfully and won the domain rights from people whose sole intent in owning the sites is to sell them at high prices.

Don't obsess over getting the perfect .com – that is, unless you are a .com. If the Internet is not your primary distribution channel, your business may do just as well with a slightly modified domain name or a .net with a little search engine optimization. In fact, depending on your business, you may be better off buying some generic domain names that describe your service or product. For example, buffalolandscaping.com instead of harryslandscaping.com for Harry's Landscaping in Buffalo, NY.

Find your Domain Name

FREE! with every Domain Name

Enter Domain Name

apple

E.g. myname.com

› Whois Lookup   › Help me choose
› Transfer

Choose your Extension   [View All]

☑ com   ☐ net   ☐ org   ☐ info
☐ biz   ☐ mobi   ☐ us   ☐ co.uk
☐ in   ☐ asia   ☐ eu   ☐ tv

Search Now

✓ 1 Email Account
✓ Privacy Protection
✓ DNS Service
✓ Domain Forwarding
✓ Mail Forwarding
View All ⇨

Domain Pricing Details

.com	$9.88	.net	$9.88	.org	$9.88	.info	$9.88
.biz	$9.88	.mobi	$19.88	.us	$9.88	.co.uk	$6.88
.in	$3.88 SALE!	.asia	$6.88 SALE!	.eu	$5.88 SALE!	.tv	$34.88

Choose from the following Domain Names

✗	apple.com		Whois	Backorder	Acquire

Stuck? Crowdsource your name

Naming your company can be challenging and time consuming. If you get writers block in coming up with a name, try crowdsourcing it online. Get **20-150** creative name suggestions from designers and writers around the world for **$200** on CrowdSpring.com. CrowdSpring's community of more than **75,000** creatives will suggest hundreds of memorable, creative, and relevant names - without breaking the bank.

Create a Tagline

Now that you have a few solid name ideas, go back to your customer-focused value proposition, your brand promise, brand values, and some of the adjectives you selected to create a tagline that explains what makes your business great.

Here are a few examples of good, explicit taglines:

FedEx: The world on time
BMW: The ultimate driving machine
Budweiser: The king of beers
eBay: The world's online marketplace

Brainstorm Touch Points & Sources of Authority

Now that you've created a brand and a message, the question is: How are you going to get your message out to your customers? That's where touch points come in. Touch points are simply opportunities to get your brand in front of your customer – whether it's through a person who is endorsing your brand (like a salesperson at a store), an ad (like a billboard or magazine ad), or other creative means. Here are some examples of typical touch points:

- Website
- Print mail
- E-mails
- Billboards
- Pens with your logo
- Vehicle lettering/wrap
- Coasters
- Key chains

Case study: FETCH

The most effective touch points come in delightful and unexpected places. World-renown branding firm Landor developed a brand, name, touch points, and style guide for a community project in Cincinnati called FETCH, one number to call for all the cabs in Cincinnati.

There are hundreds of individual operators and cab companies in Cincinnati – and finding a cab on a busy night can be difficult. It's typical for Cincinnatians who use cabs to have several numbers for individual cabs written down or stored in their cell phone – and getting a cab is an exercise in patience. On a busy night, a Cincinnatian may call five different numbers, only to get five busy signals. The FETCH team created a single routing number to all the cab companies in town that routes callers to the first non-busy number, making getting a cab faster and easier.

We started by **identifying** our three **target customer segments**, the Downtowner, the Bar Hopper, and the Traveler.

The Downtowner is a resident of downtown in their 20s and 30s who relies on public transportation and walking to accomplish most errands and activities. The Downtowner is looking for consistent, reliable transportation.

The Bar Hopper is a young professional with a spontaneous and adventurous nature who is eager to have fun and enjoy life. The Bar Hopper wants an affordable, easy, and guilt-free way to get home at the end of the evening, without the hassle of having to plan ahead.

The Traveler is a visitor to the city, unfamiliar with the area and attractions, who wants to enjoy the visit and experience the local flavor. The Traveler needs a trusted source to help navigate the city and avoid the confusion and frustration of being lost in a new place.

Next, we made a list of all the places where we might find each of our target customer segments. Then, we visualized each of those places and brainstormed a list of **touch points**:

1. **objects** in those places that could be somehow branded
2. **people** in those places who might interact with our target customer

Downtowner Places & Touch Points:
- **Home** – Refrigerator magnet, CityBeat magazine, Fountain Square billboard, signs in public elevators, doorman
- **Work** – Administrative assistant, office newsletter, bulletin board, new hire packet
- **Restaurant** – Hostess, coasters, menu ads, check tray, bathroom stalls
- **Bar** – Cab stands, welcome mats, bartender, musical acts, cigarette machines, cocktail napkins, bathroom stalls, wristbands, party favors, urinal cakes

Bar Hopper Places & Touch Points:
- **Work** – Cell phone advertising, key chains, office newsletter, new hire packet
- **Bar** - Cab stands, welcome mats, bartender, musical acts, cigarette machines, cocktail napkins, bathroom stalls, wristbands, party favors, urinal cakes
- **Restaurant** - Hostess, coasters, menu ads, check tray, bathroom stalls
- **Suburbia** – Refrigerator magnet, CityBeat magazine, billboards, radio ads, television ads

Traveler Places & Touch Points:
- **Hotel** – pens, wakeup call, concierge, tour guides, welcome basket, event planners, brochures, cab stands, room keys, bag tag, hotel television
- **Attractions** – convention center, museums, sports stadiums, music arenas, zoo, theaters
- **Restaurant/Bar** – hostess, coasters, menu ads, check tray, bathroom stalls, cab stands, welcome mats, bartender, music acts, cigarette machines, cocktail napkins, bathroom stalls, wristbands, party favors, urinal cakes
- **Airport** – baggage claim, airport shuttle, radio ads, kiosks, visitors guide, tram

Brainstorm your Touch Points

1. Make a list of the places where your customer segments live, work, and play. Where do they spend time?
2. What objects are around them in each of those places? Is there an opportunity to put your brand on any of those objects?

Brainstorm your Sources of Authority

For FETCH, sources of authority include the Visitor's Bureau, hotel and restaurant managers, the Chamber of Commerce, the city mayor, meeting planners, police, cab companies, and the press. These are key individuals and groups whose endorsement – or even mention – of the service would help get the word out to potential customers.

Brainstorm wrap-up

That wraps it up for the brainstorm. Make sure to thank your friends for all their ideas and feedback and save all the materials you've created as part of the process – we'll use these later to create a design brief for your designer to create your logo, website, and other marketing materials.

Get Feedback on Names & Taglines

Create 10 index cards with your five best name ideas and your five best taglines written out neatly. Get some feedback from friends, family, and people you trust who are outside of your brainstorming group. If appropriate, ask potential customers. First, tell them what your business does — using the customer-focused value proposition you developed. Ask them to select the best name and tagline.

1. Do they know what the product/service is just from the name without needing more information?
2. What thoughts — good and bad — do each of the names and taglines bring to mind?
3. Which do name do they like best? Which tagline?

After they've selected their favorite names and taglines, do the same exercise with five to 10 touch points. Which ones are their favorites (most delightful, unexpected)?

Design Brief

Our Company: "We sell _____ to _____ "

Name

_____

Tagline _____

Our Target Customer (needs, demographics, etc)

_____

Our Competitors' Brand, Features & Customer Needs Addressed

_____

Customer-focused Value Proposition

Features of our offering _____

Customer benefits of features _____

Dramatic difference from competitors _____

Credibility/Reason to believe us _____

Brand Identity (Personality)

Car _____

Celebrity _____

Animal _____

Spokesperson _____

Adjectives & Values

_____

Touch points

Place: _____ Touch points: _____

Place: _____ Touch points: _____

Place: _____ Touch points: _____

Design Implementation

Rule number one in design implementation: Do NOT design your logo yourself! Everyone can tell. Hire a professional designer to develop a polished design; otherwise, the message to the customer is, "We're not professionals" or "I'm not serious about this."

Our reaction to design is highly emotional. People process design at three different levels: visceral, behavioral, and reflective. Visceral design is that initial reaction to a design. Behavioral design refers to the total experience of using a product – how it looks, feels, tastes, smells, and performs. Lastly, our reflective reaction takes into account our thoughts about the design, the image it portrays, and the message it tells others about the owner's taste.

Design implementation takes into account elements such as shape, color, materials, finish, and fonts - which directly and subliminally communicate a company's values and personality through compelling imagery and design style. Properly implemented, this results in an emotional connection between the brand and the consumer.

For example, Home Depot uses color – orange – and consistently applies it to all its brand materials. Starbucks uses black and white icons. Nike uses the swoosh symbol.

Create your design brief

Synthesize your customer research, competitor research, value proposition, brand identity, name, tagline, and touch points for your designer into a single document called a **design brief**. They can use this to develop your logo, fonts, colors, website, and other marketing pieces.

Whether hiring a designer locally or hiring one online, you want to make sure that you have a clear, concise, and visual executive summary of your brand.

Color and Emotion

Given the values and adjectives you would use to describe your brand, what colors, fonts, and imagery communicate your message best? Does seeing red bring to mind passion or anger? Does blue inspire trust, calm, or depression? How we feel influences how we see colors. From infancy when our eyes first perceive colors, we start to formulate color associations that carry through adulthood.

Do no make the mistake of choosing colors or fonts based on your personal preference – instead make your color choices based on

1. what message you are trying to communicate with your brand (trust, creativity, fun, etc.)
2. the demographics of your target market (age, gender, income, etc.)

Colors 101

Blue	Constant, trustworthy, quiet, serene, dependable, reliable, committed, cool, sky, water, intellectual, calm, confident, corporate, restful, soothing, power, credibility, authority, serious
Green	Soothing, nature, refreshing, fresh, healing, pleasant, grass, spring, renewal, elegant, pine, forest, money, prestige, security, healthy
Yellow	Warm, sunny, luminous, splendor, optimistic, creative, encouraging, imaginative, enlightenment, heat, well-being, cheerful, mellow, soft, happy, sweet, citrus, sun-baked
Orange	Vital, glowing, vivid, intense, playful, expressive, happy, childlike, comedic, loud, warmth, citrus *Peach, apricot, coral, melon* - upscale, affluent, nurturing, approachable
Red	Passionate, aggressive, fast, exciting, provocative, dynamic, sexy, seductive *Winetones* – rich, refined, expensive, mature, lush, authoritative, opulent, elegant
Pink	Romantic, youthful, feminine, intense, moody, happy, sweet, high energy, vivid, shocking, wild, fun, exciting, faddish, immature, artificial, tacky, dazzling
Purple	Regal, spiritual, elegant, mysterious, complex, creative, eccentric, enigma, contemplative, sensual *Grayed* – sophisticated, subtle, soft, *Lavender* – delicate, refined, floral
Black	Powerful, mysterious, strong, classic, elegant, opaque, dark, sophisticated, style, dynamic, expensive, ominous, mourning, Mafia, occult, foreboding, durable, solid
Brown	Rich, earth, rustic, sheltering, hearth, home, substance, stability, brick, clay, terra cotta, rooted, protective, secure, dirty, leather, grains, wholesome, organic, chocolate
Neutral	Timeless, natural, classic, quality, quiet, beige, dependability, durability, time, antiquity, solid, enduring, permanence, safe, non-offensive
White	Pure, bright, lightweight, pristine, innocent, simplicity, brilliant, clarity, clean, hygiene, health, minimalist

Spark ideas for color combinations

Colorsontheweb.com provides a virtually unlimited set of designer-created color combinations. This site is guaranteed to spark some ideas in a matter of a few clicks.

Find the perfect font online

Typography is an art and a science, so you probably want to get an expert opinion from your designer. Get some ideas for what fonts are out there by browsing through over 10,000 fonts on Dafont.com.

Find reasonably priced stock images on the web

iStockphoto.com has millions of professional stock photographs, illustrations, and vector art for as little as $10 per license. If you need professional photographs of a businessman, fresh produce, a spa, a mountain, or a waterfall – you'll find thousands of choices online - and avoid spending thousands on custom photography.

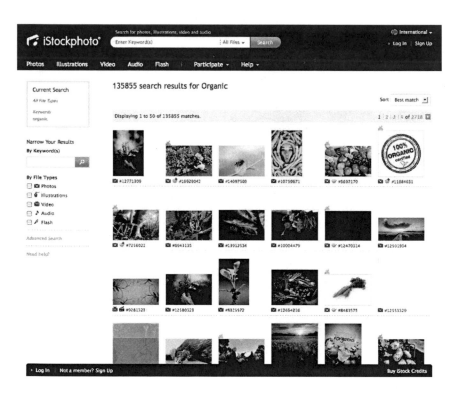

Hiring a Designer: Find the best for less

Now that you have a firm grasp of your brand identity, name, tagline, brand promise, and ideas for colors that might help communicate your message, it's time to put that research into action.

Designers are communicators who use the visual arts as their mode of communication. By listening to the message, mood, adjectives, and values of your brand, designers bring the brand to life in colors, lines, textures, and tones.

Great design comes at a price. In the next section, we'll talk about how to manage the design process to make sure you get exactly what you want – and how to keep your design costs low.

Crowdsourcing

Crowdsourcing is the lowest cost option for most kinds of graphical and web design. The word crowdsourcing comes from a combination of the wisdom of **crowds** and out**sourcing**. Crowdsourcing literally means "to outsource work to a crowd of people." By posting specific tasks on sites such as CrowdSpring.com and offering a prize for the best work, crowdsourcing sites are able to reduce the cost and increase the quality of work.

Logo, print, and web design on CrowdSpring

For logo design, web design, business cards, letterhead, and other essential startup design needs, Crowdspring.com offers well-thought-out concepts and well-executed design work at bargain-basement prices.

For $200 you can get 50-100 logo design concepts from designers from around the world, compared with $2,000-$5,000 for a typical designer to design three to five concepts.

To crowdsource a design project like a logo on Crowdspring.com, simply post a description of what you're looking for, a prize amount (example, $300) and a time limit (seven to 14 days). The posting is then viewed by thousands of freelance designers who compete for the prize money by posting designs. The site also allows you to communicate with the individual designers and request changes and adjustments to their designs, making sure that you get exactly what you're looking for. When the time is up, select your favorite design and award the prize.

Crowdspring has a community of over 75,000 creatives who compete to offer the best design. For an average $500 project, you may receive 100 design concepts.

Crowdspring takes care of the Non Disclosure Agreement and Intellectual Property Agreement so that you own your designs free and clear.

Time Frame: 7-14 Days
Cost (suggested): Logo $300-$600, Website $1,000

Tips for Crowdsourcing designs

1. Pay a little extra for a private project. You don't want your logo design project showing up in search engines.
2. Require an NDA (use CrowdSpring's). You're going to be disclosing your design brief and a good amount of valuable research in order to get quality design and you want to make sure it remains confidential.
3. Set a good award amount. A higher award means more participation and better designs.
4. When you post your design summary, include the relevant pieces of your design brief. Make sure the most important points are typed into CrowdSpring's questionnaire, but feel free to upload additional materials.
5. Promote the project. Once you've posted your project, check for similar projects on CrowdSpring. Identify the entries you like and reach out to those designers directly, letting them know that you like their work and that you'd like them to participate in your project.
6. When you get entries, make sure to score them immediately and provide feedback. If you really like a design, but need some changes, tell the designer exactly what you'd like them to change. If they feel that they are in the running for the award, they will generally make the changes within 24 hours.
7. Get input from outside. It's going to be a tough choice! Get your friends to weigh in on their favorite designs – they may see things that you don't. CrowdSpring also allows you to open your project up to a vote, getting the feedback from the general public.
8. Get the file types you need. Make sure that you get Vector (original, high quality) files as well as high-resolution (big) and low-resolution (small) JPG versions. Keep in mind that with logos, you may need black-and-white or inverse versions of your logo for dark and light backgrounds.

Find a local designer with Behance.net

Behance.net is a network of graphic designers, industrial designers, and web designers around the globe who keep portfolios of their work and their designs online. Behance.net allows you to search for designers by city, meaning that you can find talented designers in your local area and browse their portfolios before you contact them.

The designers on Behance vary widely in terms of rates and experience. Some of the designers on Behance have designed products, brands, and ad campaigns for multiple Fortune 500 companies and have years of experience in branding and design. Others are talented freelancers right out of college.

If you see some work you like, click through and contact the designer directly and ask for a quote or just set up a meeting. You'll want to interview a couple designers to make sure that you not only like their work, but that you'll like working with them as well.

Things to consider when hiring a local designer

1. What is their hourly rate (how do they charge)?
2. How long will the project take?
3. How many initial concepts you will get?
4. Who will own the intellectual property (you want to own your designs, meaning that you want the trademark rights and copyrights to the designs)
5. Do they "get" the brand and the message?
6. Do you feel a creative chemistry with this person? Do they have great ideas for touch points, ad campaigns, etc.?
7. You'll likely be working with this person quite a bit over the years – do they have the ability to deliver all that you'll need – logo, sales brochures, posters, ad campaigns, etc?

Cost (varies greatly): $2,000-$7,000
Time Frame (varies greatly): 2 weeks - 2 months

Get feedback on design concepts

Poll your closest friends and family over e-mail, Facebook, or text before you select your logo. Don't spam all your contacts – just get feedback from a diverse group (age, gender, etc.) that you trust and who understand your business. Do they see something that you don't see?

Don't feel compelled to take a vote or make a decision by committee – just get their thoughts on the different concepts. Ultimately, it's up to you.

Be consistent in messaging and design execution

Make sure that when you are delivering your message that your brand identity (who I am), value proposition (what I can do for you), brand promise (my promise to you), target audience (who I'm talking to), and touch points (how my message is delivered) are consistent every time.

Brand consistency involves the communication of messages in a way that doesn't take away from the core brand proposition. While certain aspects of branding might change, the core message shouldn't change. For example, the Apple logo has changed numerous times since Apple was founded. However, Apple's brand proposition – to create innovative, high-quality, great-looking computer products – has never changed.

7   Marketing, Advertising, & Publicity

"If I was down to my last dollar, I'd spend it on public relations."
— *Bill Gates*

Now that you've created a business model and a brand, it's time to get the word out about your business through publicity, advertising, search engine optimization, and word-of-mouth marketing.

In the previous chapter, we talked about touch points — all the opportunities you have to get your brand in front of customers through branded objects and people who are advocates for your business.

Now we're going to talk about creating a message for your press releases and advertisements. Once you create that message, we'll walk through a step-by-step process for creating and distributing a press release. Then we'll explore different types of advertising such as TV, radio, newspapers, magazines, and online advertising.

Next, we'll explore the basics of search engine optimization (SEO), social media, and word of mouth (or viral) marketing. From setting up an e-mail marketing campaign to creating a viral video campaign and driving traffic through social media, we're going to cover every aspect of online marketing.

Finally, we'll explore business development and customer relationship management (CRM) tools for those businesses that have direct contact with a targeted base of customers. These tools will help you manage the strategic sales process and coordinate multiple sales reps.

As an advertiser and promoter, you need to ask yourself "Where are my customers looking all day?" Chances are they're checking out Facebook or Google, watching television, or reading the Sunday paper. Or maybe your customers are low-tech or spend most of their time driving and listening to the radio. Put yourself in their shoes and try to envision different ways you can reach out to them.

Getting the Word Out: Publicity vs. Advertising

"There's no such thing as public opinion – only published opinion."
– Winston Churchill

Public Relations (PR) or publicity is media attention that includes newspaper articles, magazine reviews, TV reports, blog posts, etc., about your business.

Publicity is essentially free advertising and, depending on the news outlet, can generate a lot of attention. Publicity like articles and reviews are generally more credible than advertisements because they are written by a third party such as an expert or a reporter.

This is why positive publicity and press coverage is priceless. Reporters are unbiased, independent third-party experts, so their opinions are highly valued by consumers.

The downside to publicity is that you can't control the message. When a reporter decides to do an article on your business, they may already have an angle in mind – which they may or may not share with you during the course of an interview.

Press releases are news articles written by you, which means that you have a little more control over the message, but many times press releases are just a starting point. Reporters use press releases for details and ideas for articles.

When you issue a press release, reporters may choose not to publish your press release, but instead may write their own articles with a different angle. In such cases, they'll usually reach out to you directly for an interview. Another downside of press releases is that most articles are text only (no images), which limits brand awareness.

Advertising puts you in control of the message and the mode of distribution, but it's not free. The benefit of advertising is that unlike publicity, you can buy as much awareness and attention as you want – the sky is limit. While newspapers and magazines may tire of writing articles about how great your product is, they will always take your advertising money.

Most media outlets make their money on advertising, which can be expensive. The benefit to advertising is that it gives you a richer connection with your customers, allowing you to speak directly to them and visually reinforce your brand in your ad. Advertising agencies specialize in designing messages and ad designs that will surprise, delight, and interest consumers with a single image or 30 seconds of film.

Creating a Message That Sticks

Even though your business is in its infancy and doesn't have much history or brand awareness yet, we need to create a story about your company that you want the press and your potential customers to talk about for years to come.

Messaging is about creating context, surprise, interest, credibility, a reason to care, and a reason to act.

Dan and Chip Heath's must-read book on messaging, "Made to Stick," outlines how to create a message that sticks in people's minds. They delve into a broad range of psychological concepts and break down in easy-to-understand components the recipe for success in creating a message that sticks.

The recipe for sticky messages is simple, and comes with a cool acronym (SUCCES):
- Simple – Be clear and concise
- Unexpected – Get people to pay attention
- Concrete – Help them understand and remember
- Credible – Make them believe and agree
- Emotional – Give them a reason to care
- Stories – Show them with examples how they should act

We'll tackle a few of those now. To begin, go back to your Customer Focused Value Proposition in the Branding chapter and pick out the single most important element of your value proposition to customers.

Then, from that same Customer Focused Value Proposition, list all of your sources of credibility – the reasons to believe. These are two elements we will use to start crafting your message.

Example:

Customer focused value proposition: *GlowCycle's Glow-in-the-Dark Paint illuminates your bicycle and prevents you from being hit by cars in the dark.*

The key here is to keep the value proposition very **simple** and obvious. It should be short and to the point – it "prevents you from being hit by a car" not "with over 10 colors of glow in the dark paint, anyone can make their bike glow at night and increase their bike's visibility and style on the road."

Sources of credibility: *Developed by a Tour de France-winning cyclist who was hit by a car while training at night.*

There are two **sources of authority** here – a traditional authority like a medal-winning professional cyclist, but also an antiauthority. An antiauthority is an average person that people identify with. Anti-authorities speak directly to our emotions in a way that makes us feel like "that could have been me."

Now we need to take this simple, credible message and add a story – some spice that will **surprise** and **interest** readers and viewers. In order to do that, we'll have to **break a pattern**.

"Glow in the Dark Bike Hits Car at 60mph – Driver Walks Away Uninjured"

We'll, that might be a little too much. But you get the picture – the headline of the message should be a little surprising. In this case, we broke a pattern because most people would expect a story about how a biker was hit by a car – not the other way around! Here's a more positive one that could be used for a newsworthy promotional piece:

"Glow in the Dark Cyclist Makes 200-Mile Ride Overnight"

The unexpected is a powerful source of surprise and interest. Have you ever been on a Southwest Airlines flight where the flight attendants sing a hilarious song about the pre-flight safety check while they show you where the exits are and how to buckle your seatbelt? Their goal is not just to delight customers – it's also to get people to pay attention and remember important safety information.

Another way to create interest is to add a little **mystery**. Can you imagine this local news story?

"On our News at 6, Paula Amuto talks to police about the bicyclist who was hit by a taxi in Greenwood. <u>Find out which cities have the worst fatalities</u> for bicyclists…"

Right now that viewer is thinking, "I wonder if *my* city is one of the most dangerous for bicycling." They are curious and waiting to find out the answer.

Next, we're going to need to come up with some **facts** that will give **context** to your story and help people understand and remember. Here are some facts about melanoma that help give the disease a little context – and may also be a little surprising.

"Melanoma accounts for 4% of skin cancers but 80% of skin cancer deaths. It affects the young and old. It is the <u>No. 1 cancer killer</u> of young women."

By explaining how melanoma compares with other skin cancers (it's more deadly) and by ranking it with other cancers (it's a high risk for young women especially), the disease now has more context in the reader's mind and is easier to understand and easier to remember. With this context and memory established in the reader's mind, the next time they hear about melanoma, they are more likely to pay attention.

Context helps people understand your story – and understanding helps them remember. The best example of this principle is the analogy given by Dan and Chip Heath in "Made to Stick."

Try this experiment:
Think of as many white things as you can in 10 seconds. How many did you come up with? Probably not that many. Well, let's add some context: your refrigerator.

Try to think of as many white things *in your refrigerator* as you can in 10 seconds.

Chances are that you'll come up with more ideas because your refrigerator is a concrete point of reference in your imagination. So, you'll think of milk, cheese, half and half, eggs, leftover jasmine rice, and ice cream.

Analogies, metaphors, associations, details, statistics, and examples all help to provide concreteness and context for your story.

Putting **real people** and **emotion** into the story helps bring it to life. Add these human interest elements to your story to help people identify with you. Don't go overboard with sensational details, but try to use real examples and quotes from experts (authorities) and real people (anti-authorities) who your readers would identify with.

"Carrie was 18 when she was diagnosed with melanoma. She was absolutely beautiful and so fun to be around. She loved to be tan and I worried that she would have wrinkles when she got to be my age, but I never knew skin cancer could kill someone so young," said mother Karen Shelby, a library assistant at Williams South school.

Wow. Not only is that real, it's packed with emotion: love, regret, and grief. Karen and Carrie's story is memorable because it's about real people. Here's another:

John Churchill, avid amateur cyclist and high school teacher, bicycled 200 miles overnight in the dark on Saturday on the fifth anniversary of the injury that kept him in a coma for two weeks. Churchill was hit by a car while cycling on a road at dusk in 2005. Using special Glow In the Dark Paint made by GlowCycle, he made the trek safely Saturday without incident.

"I train everyday and usually at night. I love cycling, but I'm well aware of the dangers. I do everything that I can now to make sure that cars can see me on the road," said Churchill.

Creating a Message

Unexpected

- You'd never expect to see this...
- Here's the shocking truth...
- What people will be surprised to learn...
- Here's the mystery...

Concrete

- Here's a simple analogy...
- Let me put this number in context...
- Here's a tangible example...
- We're going to show you (make it visual)...

Credible

- We know what we're talking about because...
  - o We have experts!
  - o We have data!
  - o We can show you!
  - o We've won awards!

Emotional

- You should care because...
- Here's why people will identify with this...

Stories

- Here's a story of how this worked for one person...
- Here's how this could have helped this person...

Do-it-Yourself Publicity

Press releases are news articles written by you, the business owner, to communicate the start of a new business or the launch of a new product to the news media. Press releases are used by media outlets everywhere – from city and state newspapers to national publications such as the Wall Street Journal – and can help you drive awareness of your brand through publicity.

To begin leveraging these news sources to get an audience, you'll want to start building relationships with specific reporters, bloggers, and other media representatives who cover your topic or locale.

Getting Local and National Media Attention

Make a list of all your target newspapers, websites, TV stations and radio stations. Search their websites for the contact information of specific reporters who cover your topic area (health, local business, politics, entertainment, etc) and start to build relationships with those reporters. Start reading their articles and tuning in to their segments so that you can get a feel for what types of stories they look for.

If possible, find out what their deadline is and when their editorial meetings are. *Editorial meetings* are used to plan upcoming stories and *deadlines* are the last day that you can submit a press release or a reporter can submit a story.

Introduce yourself and your company well in advance of your launch and ask them if they would be interested in covering the launch of your company.

Reporters love exclusive stories, so start with the largest publications and stations first and offer an exclusive story (meaning that you will only talk to them). As you get closer to launch, plan a schedule of press releases, TV appearances, and interviews with each news outlet's deadline in mind.

How to Create Your Own Press Release

A press release should read like a New York Times news article – straightforward, no fluff, no exclamation points, no hyperbole. It is written in the third person, meaning that it should sound like every other news article – no "I," "you," or "we" (except in quotes) – just "it," "they," "she," and "he."

Sentences and paragraphs should be short, with about three or four lines per paragraph. Write in active voice with strong verbs: "The Mayor was shocked by the ruling," not "The Mayor exhibited surprise over the ruling."

First, identify your newsworthy news. Don't be afraid to toot your own horn; this is a huge opportunity to promote your business and raise awareness for your brand. If your company has reached a milestone, celebrated an anniversary, launched a new product, opened a new location, hired a new CEO, or received an award, shout it from the rooftops – it's a good excuse to be in the news.

Successes like significant growth, major milestones, and new partnerships not only promote your success, they build credibility and could lead to new customers.

Knowledge is king. If you don't have anything newsworthy to report at the moment, write a release that offers readers "tips" or help in your field of expertise. For instance, share survey results or a top 10 list.

Events are also newsworthy. Are you hosting a fundraiser, a dinner, conference or other event? Be aware of TV visuals, photo ops, and rich media opportunities. For instance, if you're opening a new store or location, have a Grand Opening and invite local TV and radio stations to report live on location.

Real Example Press Release

MEDIA ALERT: EMBARGOED UNTIL 8 PM WEDNESDAY, SEPTEMBER 22 - Winners will not be notified prior to event.

Cincinnati Innovates Awards Announced

Event Venue Booking Website, Safer Tool for Root Canals, Predictor for Osteoporosis are Top Winners

Cincinnati, OH (PRWeb) September 22, 2010 - Cincinnati Innovates wrapped up its four-month online competition Wednesday by recognizing 10 winners in the regional innovation competition.

Awards were given at a ceremony Wednesday night at the Freedom Center in downtown Cincinnati. Nearly 300 people attended the event along with 24 corporate sponsors and members of the Greater Cincinnati Venture Association.

Top prize of $25,000 went to Jocelyn Cates, who entered an event venue booking website application called Venue Agent.

Cates was driven to create VenueAgent after working with brides to book venues for their weddings. VenueAgent helps brides and event planners find available venues – and allows venues to promote discounts for off-peak and off-season dates.

"Many brides don't know that booking on a Thursday or Friday could save them 50% on their venue – and many venues have a tough time selling off-season dates. VenueAgent is like the Hotels.com of event venues," she says.

Cates was among 301 people who completed online entry forms at www.cincinnatiinnovates.com. Thirty-four percent were women, and 17 self-identified ethnic groups were represented. More than 16,000 votes were cast for the HYPE! Community Choice Award.

The competition was open to anyone with an idea or an invention who has a connection to the Greater Cincinnati and Northern Kentucky MSA.

"The purpose of Cincinnati Innovates is to identify high potential entrepreneurs and technologies and connect them with more than 50 local resources for entrepreneurs," says Elizabeth Edwards, former venture capital investor and founder of Metro Innovation, a catalyst for innovation and entrepreneurship.

The competition was produced by Metro Innovation, with partners Taft law firm, public-private venture capital firm CincyTech, the Northern Kentucky eZone, and 22 other area sponsors.

"This year we really saw more winners than we had awards to give out," said attorney James Zimmerman, a partner at Taft. "From biotechnology and the Internet to consumer products, medical devices and green technology, the range of innovation has been amazing."

Bob Coy, president of CincyTech, says the competition helps spur local entrepreneurial activity, which then spurs economic growth.

"We've been very pleased with the kinds of participants Cincinnati Innovates is attracting," said Coy. "We are looking for strong startups in which to invest, and we've seen many good ideas coming out of this competition."

About the company: Metro Innovation is a catalyst for innovation and entrepreneurship in cities around the world. More information at www.metroinnovation.com.

Contact:
Elizabeth Edwards
555-555-5555
myemail@email.com

Components of a Press Release

A press release has six main components: the headline, the summary, the dateline and lead, the body paragraphs, the company information, and the contact information of the person issuing the press release.

Headline

Examples:
- Alien Spaceship Docks at Manhattan Harbor
- Bill's Electric Donates $1 million to FoodBank
- Catholic High Schools Compete for Football State Title

A good headline provides information and is not an advertisement. It gets the reader's attention quickly and makes them want to read more.

Make sure when you craft the headline of your press release you include a keyword or two that people are likely to search in order to find your company – and always provide a link to your website as a hyperlink or full web address somewhere in the press release.

First, choose a highly searched, relevant keyword or phrase. Place that keyword or phrase near the beginning of the headline and build around it. The headline should be no more than **60-170 characters** long and less than eight words. It should be written in Title Case, with every word capitalized except for prepositions and articles that are three characters or less (of, and, at, in, etc).

Make sure that the headline summarizes the press release. When you skim a website or newspaper, it's the headlines that help you decide which articles you want to read. The same is true for search engines. The headline is the first part of a press release that search engines index, so write the headline with keyword optimization in mind.

Write your headline and summary **last**. This will save you time and ensure that the headline matches the story perfectly.

Summary

Examples:
- Alien Spaceship Docks at Manhattan Harbor
Police and National Guard are on High Alert, Waiting for Contact
- Bill's Electric Donates $1 million to FoodBank
Employee-Owned Company Believes in Giving Back During Tough Economic Times
- Catholic High Schools Compete for Football State Title
St. Matthew's and Central Catholic Will Play in the Semifinals on Friday at the Arena

The summary paragraph is a synopsis of the information contained in the release. It typically follows the headline and gives you the opportunity to provide a brief description of your business and the information you are sharing.

Some wire services and media will only display your headline, summary and a link to your press release. So, if your release does not have a summary paragraph, readers may not click through for more information.

The summary can be **one to four sentences** and should be written in Title Case. Include your company's name within the headline, summary or first few paragraphs to get your name out there right up front.

The Dateline and Lead

Example:

City, State (Wire) Day, Month, Year — the most important information you want to share.

The lead and first paragraph of a press explains the gist of the article and answers the "who, what, when, where, how, and why (anyone should care)" questions – all in **25 words or less**.

Keep the lead paragraph compelling and simple, minimizing adjectives and flowery language.

The Body Copy

This is your chance to share your news in **300-800 words**. Elaborate on the details and draw people in. Remember to keep your tone neutral and objective like a newscaster – not gimmicky like an advertisement.

Try to incorporate elements like quotes, human interest, facts, and figures that will help add flavor and interest to your piece. Quotes from customers and experts are especially powerful.

Remember to repeat your primary keyword(s) two to four times in the body of the document and include a link to your website (http://www.company.com).

Your final paragraph should summarize your main points, provide any necessary legal language, or offer a link to get more information.

Boilerplate Statement

The boilerplate statement is standard "About the Company" that you copy and paste onto almost every document

Google's Boilerplate statement:

"About Google Inc.
Google's innovative search technologies connect millions of people around the world with information every day. Founded in 1998 by Stanford Ph.D. students Larry Page and Sergey Brin, Google today is a top web property in all major global markets. Google's targeted advertising program, which is the largest and fastest growing in the industry, provides businesses of all sizes with measurable results, while enhancing the overall web experience for users. Google is headquartered in Silicon Valley with offices throughout North America, Europe, and Asia. For more information, visit www.google.com."

Contact Information

Contact information provides reporters with a way to reach you. It should include your name, company, telephone number, and e-mail address. This information is not published in the media.

Guidelines for Great Press Releases

Start strong with a brow-lifting headline and be concise. You only have a matter of seconds to grab your readers' attention and not long to hold it. Use active voice and strong verbs.

Identify your company within the first few paragraphs. Link to your website and include relevant keywords in the press release to help with SEO.

Tell a story and use real life examples.

Write professionally - no hype, slang, exclamation points or spelling mistakes. These hurt credibility. Write your release in Word. Use spell check. Print out your press release and read it aloud to proofread it. Most media outlets don't proofread press releases before publishing – that's your job.

Be clear and use ordinary language. Don't use jargon – you will confuse or lose your audience.

Why should anyone care? Include information that is timely, highlights something new or unusual, and is useful to your audience. Offer "tips" in your field of expertise. Pick an angle and tie your information to current events, recent studies, trends and social issues. This makes your message more timely and relevant.

Avoid clichés like "great customer service" and focus on what makes you truly unique. Don't exaggerate, just stick to the facts.

Attach files like images, video, and links that will capture the attention of your readers. Attach logos, headshots, product shots, photographs, audio files, video files, etc.

Distributing a National Press Release

BusinessWire and PR Newswire are is the largest PR
distribution companies in the U.S. They reach thousands of major
newspapers, websites, television stations, radio stations, and
journals. For the most widespread media attention you can get,
these two wire services will be your best options, but also the most
expensive – costing up to **$500 per press release**. BusinessWire
also allows you to target your release to specific regions or media
formats so you pay only for the regions and formats you want.

More and more readers – and traditional reporters – get their news
from the Internet. **PRWeb** allows you to upload and send a press
release to online distribution channels such as Google News and
Yahoo News for as little as **$90 per press release.** With more and
more media looking to the Internet for their news, PRWeb offers a
cheap, fast solution for startups – and a lot of helpful hints.

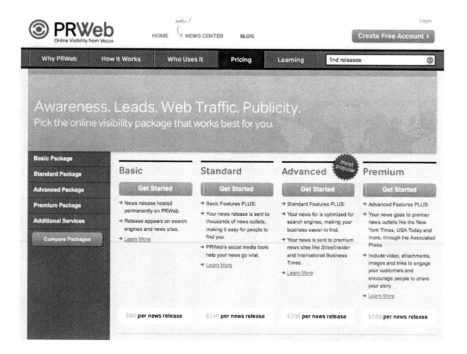

Reporters Looking for Stories

HARO (Help a Reporter Out) is a posting service for bloggers and reporters looking for stories on different topics. Sign up for the daily e-mails of hundreds of story requests from around the world at www.helpareporter.com. Be on the look out for reporters and bloggers who write for mainstream media or for niche blogs that are relevant to your business. If your product or service fits within the reporter's criteria, reach out to them with a pitch.

Two Types of Advertising

Image or awareness advertising seeks to build awareness of a brand over time, establishing the brand's values and benefits in the minds of consumers. Most TV commercials and magazine ads for makeup, fashion, or consumer products are focused on raising brand awareness.

An example of awareness advertising is a perfume commercial that just shows the perfume, a model or two, then the brand name and tagline. This serves to remind the consumer that the perfume exists and that it's desirable. This is distinguished from direct response marketing, which is associated with an immediate call to action, such as a limited time offer of a free makeup bag with purchase of the perfume.

Direct-response marketing (DRM) is a type of advertising designed to drive an immediate action. That action could take the form of calling an 800 number, sending in a postcard to renew a subscription, signing up to receive free information, or making a purchase. Unlike image and awareness advertising, the results of direct-response marketing are specific, traceable, and quantifiable.

One type of DRM is a coupon that arrives through direct mail or e-mail. Coupons are a measurable form of DRM because advertisers are able to track the response to the piece of mail using the barcode on the coupon. When the customer makes a purchase and uses the coupon, the code is logged so that the retailer can track the number of people who responded to the offer.

Drivers of Effective Advertisements

Five factors determine the effectiveness of an advertisement: quality of the message, number of impressions, quality of the media channel, target audience, and timeliness.

1. Quality of the message

If you spend $1 million on a 30 second spot during the Superbowl, but no one can figure out what the ad is for, you're in trouble. The message should be simple, unexpected, concrete, credible, and well designed. The quality of the print design or video production matters because it speaks to the quality of your brand.

2. Number of impressions

For print media, the number of impressions is driven by circulation, or how many people subscribe to a newspaper or magazine. For radio, it's the number of listeners and for television, the number of viewers.

Media channels vary greatly in terms of the number of people they reach. For instance, a local access cable channel reaches very few viewers compared with HBO. The number of viewers or listeners changes depending on the time of day. The number of radio listeners peaks at rush hour when people are driving to and from work. The number of television viewers peaks in the evening and during special events like the Superbowl. Newspapers tend to have more Sunday subscribers and many magazines have special holiday issues.

3. Quality of media channel

Media channels vary widely in terms of the richness and type of interaction with the customer. Television is an intensely rich form of media because it involves sight, sound, and movement. The Internet is a highly interactive form of media.

4. Target audience

Different media channels have different target audiences. MTV draws a completely different kind of viewer than ABC. Find out what percentage of the viewers or readers of a certain media are your exact target customers.

If you are marketing a niche product to fishermen, a national magazine like TIME is not as targeted as a specialty magazine like Bassmaster Magazine. Even though TIME has a circulation of more than 3 million and Bassmaster has a circulation of only half a million, you know that 100% of Bassmaster readers are interested in fishing.

5. Timeliness of the ad

Timeliness applies mostly to seasonal products and events, like Christmas sales and summer vacation destinations. Staple products such as toilet paper are needed all year long, so timeliness is less of a factor.

Common Advertising Terms

CPI: Cost per impression
CPM: Cost per thousand impressions – Used for all types of advertising
CPC: Cost per click through – Used for online advertising

CPA: Cost per action – Used for opt-in email advertising and other direct response marketing

CPS: Cost per sale – Calculated internally as a metric to track advertising effectiveness across multiple media channels

Advertising Costs

Advertising costs are measured apples to apples across different media channels, such as print, television, and the Internet by CPM. In advertising CPM stands for cost per mille, or cost per thousand, and refers to how much you are spending per 1,000 impressions. An impression is when a viewer sees an ad.

It can be difficult to quantify what a good CPM is because different media outlets have different audiences. For example, advertising on a travel website likely would have a much higher value for a hotel or airline than a toy or a game.

Make a list of all the magazines, television shows, radio stations, newspapers, websites, blogs, and billboards your target customer might read. Search for each publication's **media kit** or **rate card**. This will tell you the number of impressions the media gets in terms of circulation, viewership (or Nielsen rating), or traffic. Then look for the cost of the advertisement. In order to compare the different forms of media, we'll need to calculate the CPM of each publication.

Calculating CPM

1. Determine the cost of the advertising and how many impressions the ad will make.

2. Divide the cost of the ad campaign by the number of impressions to find the cost per impression. For example, if the ad cost $200

and would be seen 25,000 times, you would divide $200 by 25,000 to get $0.008.

3. Multiply the cost per impression by 1,000 to calculate the CPM. So to finish this example, you would multiply $0.008 by 1,000 to find the CPM is $8.

Calculating the Total Cost of Advertising

Calculate the total cost of advertising by adding up the cost of the ad space and the cost of production. For instance, if you're producing a television commercial, find the cost of the commercial spot by searching on SRDS or calling the TV station and then get a quote from a local video production company on how much it would cost to produce a 30 second commercial (30 seconds is standard).

The cost of the ad space largely depends on the number of impressions – which could be viewers in the case of TV, listeners in the case of radio, and circulation in the case of newspapers and magazines. With television, Nielsen ratings are used to quantify viewers.

Cost of Ad Space = CPM Rate x (Impressions / 1,000)

Depending on the type of ad, the cost of production could include things such as print design, sign printing and installation, photography (or stock photographs), video and audio editing, models, actors, and voice talent.

Total Cost = Cost of Production + Cost of Ad Space

To give you an idea of typical circulation rates and viewership, here are some examples:

- **Bassmaster** has a circulation of roughly 500,000.
- **GQ** has a circulation of nearly 1 million.
- **TIME** Magazine's circulation is more than 3 million.
- For television, **Dancing With the Stars** drew a viewing audience of 21 million for its 2010 premier.
- The 2008 **Superbowl** had over 100 million viewers. This is why the starting price of a Superbowl ad is around $1 million.

Keep in mind that some local newsletters and magazines can have circulations as low as 10,000. If you're advertising to a targeted local area, these publications are an affordable option.

The following chart details cost estimates for a variety of advertising media. Advertising rates vary widely by how targeted the media is – and how influential. Television advertising is very broad and relatively cheap on a CPM basis, so if you have a niche business service, you will spend a lot of money marketing to an irrelevant audience. Direct mail is very targeted – whether by demographic, geography, or individual – but is much more expensive on a CPM basis.

Entry Cost: $1 versus $1 million

Direct mail, e-mail newsletters, and online CPC ads are three kinds of advertising that have a low barrier to entry; they can be organized in a matter of minutes and they can be scaled on a per impression basis.

For these three types of advertisements, you can run a single ad – send one e-mail, send one postcard, or post one CPC ad – at less than $1 in total.

Television, radio, magazines, newspapers, and billboards have a much higher starting price because each ad receives thousands of impressions.

The minimum order size for these types of ads is $500-$10,000 depending on the media.

Advertising Costs
(by type of media, rate, and impressions)

	Rates (CPM)			Impressions (Circulation/Viewers)		
				100,000	1,000,000	10,000,000
				National Niche Magazines	Magazines in the Grocery Aisle	Popular Television Shows
	Low	High	Average			
Magazine	*depends on circulation*					
National, Full Page, 4 Color	$10.00	$100.00	**$35.00**	$3,500	$35,000	$350,000
Newspaper	*depends on circulation*					
Half page, B&W	$5.00	$50.00	**$15.00**	$1,500	$15,000	$150,000
Television	*depends on viewers*					
30 sec, Primetime Network	$10.00	$60.00	**$20.00**	$2,000	$20,000	$200,000
30 sec, Primetime Cable	$5.00	$20.00	**$7.00**	$700	$7,000	$70,000
Radio	*depends on listeners*					
30 sec, Drive Time	$3.00	$20.00	**$6.00**	$600	$6,000	$60,000
Billboard	*depends on location and traffic*					
Static, Rotating, LED	$2.00	$40.00	**$20.00**	$2,000	$20,000	$200,000
Online Ads	*depends on keyword and bid*					
Google, Facebook, etc	$0.10	$20.00	**$3.00**	$300	$3,000	$30,000
Direct Mail	*depends on printing cost*					
Printing, Postage, List	$350.00	$500.00	**$400.00**	$40,000	$400,000	$4,000,000
Email Marketing	*depends on list quality*					
List, Broadcast, Analytics	$25.00	$75.00	**$30.00**	$3,000	$30,000	$300,000
Email Newsletters	*depends on email service*					
Sending & analytics only	$7.00	$12.00	**$10.00**	$1,000	$10,000	$100,000
Vehicle Wrap			**$1.00**	$2,000-$5,000 installed		

Magazines and Newspapers

To find the ad rates for newspapers and magazines, search for the publication name and the words "Rate Card" or "Media Kit" — these detail the published advertising rates for the publication by ad size, area, and special issue.

If you're having trouble finding media rates and circulation numbers or if you need more ideas of potential media outlets, for $150-$300 per month, Standard Rate and Data Services (http://www.srds.com) allows you to browse the media rates, circulation, and demographics of thousands of publishers and content providers — including magazines, newspapers, websites, TV, and radio.

Need an ad designed? Look no further than Crowdspring or Behance. Graphic designers do more than just logos. Crowdspring designers can produce professionally designed ads for as little as $500-$2,000. Make sure that your message is well defined and provide plenty of visual ideas. Your Design Brief should fully explain the values and attributes of your brand as well as your target audience and the type of publication where the ad will be shown.

Provide the size requirements of the ad (full or half page) from the magazine's media kit and any other design necessary requirements (B&W only, 4 color, etc).

Television and Radio

Television commercials could be as low as $5,000 to produce with a green screen and professional crew as long as there's no celebrity talent involved. Radio commercials are many times produced in the actual studio by the radio personalities themselves and can cost as little as $1,000 to produce.

Television markets typically cover a 75-mile radius from the stations' transmitter sites. This area called a Designated Marketing Area (DMA) and can encompass several counties and many cities.

The average television network program achieves a Nielsen rating of 11.0, which means it reaches 11% of the 114.9 million homes in America, or 12.6 million homes.

If an advertiser were to buy 10 commercials on a network with an 11.0 rating (NBC, for example), then it would make 10 times 12.6 million or 126 million impressions.

If the network charged $150,000 per 30-second commercial, the total cost of a 10-commercial schedule would be $1.5 million.

To calculate the CPM of this schedule, first take the total number of impressions and divide by 1,000.

$$= \frac{126,000,000}{1,000} = 126,000$$

To get the CPM (cost per thousand impressions), divide the cost by the number of impressions in thousands.

$$CPM = \frac{\$1,500,000}{126,000} = \$11.90$$

So, the CPM, or cost of making 1,000 impressions on that network, is $11.90.

Best Television Commercials

Comparison

Apple's "I'm a Mac and I'm a PC" campaign featured a cool, laid back younger kid as Mac and a stuffy, corporate type as PC, reinforcing Apple's brand image.

Comparisons offer the consumer an edgier message than the traditional "we're awesome" advertisement. Instead, the message is clear: We are *better* than the competition.

I'm a PC.   I'm a Mac.

Visual Concreteness

Reagan's war on drugs came with a powerful set of public service announcements, including the "This is your brain   and this is your brain on drugs" ad, which showed an egg cracked open and frying in a pan, reinforcing the idea that drugs fry your brain.   The commercial was visual, concrete, and surprising, making it both effective and memorable.

Personification

While "animals with accents" has not been recognized as a stand-alone category of advertising, it should be! The two most memorable animals in advertising, the GEICO Gecko and the Taco Bell Chihuahua, have been part of some of the most successful ad campaigns in history. The ads highlight the playful side of the two brands in a memorable and entertaining way.

Billboards

Billboards range in price depending on the type. There are three types: static (like the one shown below), rotating (mechanical strips), and electronic LED boards (these look like giant televisions).

Electronic billboards cost more than static and rotating billboards. The average CPM for a static billboard is about $2. Rotating boards have an average CPM of $5 and LED billboards run about $35-$40 CPM.

LED billboards are priced by the minute and each ad is shown for eight seconds. LED billboard ads can cost as little as $1,200 for 648 minutes (.45 days.) or as much as $50,000 for 2,520 minutes (1.75 days).

LED's are more effective than static or rotating billboards because they are animated. Unlike static billboards, they are constantly changing, which increases drivers' sensitivity to the ads and causes people to pay attention.

Online Advertising

Google Adwords, Facebook Ads Manager, and LinkedIn Direct ads are just a few examples of CPC online advertising networks. Depending on what type of product or service you are marketing and what type of audience you are marketing to, you'll want to use different types of ads and ad networks.

Banner ads are the large image-based ads that you see on the top, bottom, and sides of web pages. Text ads are like the Google ads shown below – text-only ads with a link to a website.

Online advertising is charged in two ways – either CPM (cost per thousand impressions) or CPC (cost per click).

For non-interactive media formats such as magazines and television, CPM makes sense because without a coupon code, it's difficult to track the exact response of an ad. However, with an interactive media like the Internet or email, clicks can be tracked, so take advantage of the media format and only pay for actual clicks (CPC).

Online ads can be targeted by keyword, demographic, or both. Google is the world's standard in keyword advertising, so let's start there.

1. Find keywords

To begin, use Google's keyword tool to brainstorm new keywords for your ad. This will help to identify good keywords to bid on.

Find as many keywords as you can (50+ is good) and look for keywords that receive a lot of traffic (50,000+ is good).

2. Estimate traffic

Keyword traffic refers to the number of times that people search for that keyword each month. For instance, over 30 million people globally search for the word "laptop" in a month.

Once you have a list of the keywords on Google's Keyword Tool, select the keywords you want based on their traffic and CPC and download the list into Excel. Next, use Google's Traffic Estimator Tool to estimate the traffic you could achieve given different CPC bids and daily budgets.

3. Determine your maximum CPC bid

Copy the list of keyword ideas from Excel into Google's Traffic Estimator. The tool will generate a new spreadsheet that includes the Estimated Daily Cost and Estimated Daily Clicks. Download this spreadsheet into Excel in order to complete the following calculations.

a. Calculate the average of the Estimated Daily Cost column.

b. Calculate the average of the Estimated Daily Clicks column.

c. Divide the average estimated daily cost and the average estimated daily clicks to get the average cost per click of your unique combination of keywords. This is the average CPC bid.

Now let's determine your maximum CPC bid.

Maximum CPC Bid = Gross Margin x Sales Per Click (%)

Find your unit gross margin in your Unit Economics calculations (see Feasibility chapter and Unit Economics).

Sales Per Click or *Conversion Rate* is the percentage of people who buy after clicking on your ad. Your estimated Sales Per Click is anyone's guess initially, but generally, less than 5% of people who click on an ad actually make a purchase. Your Sales Per Click could be as low as a thousandth of a percent and as high as 10%, depending on what you're selling. The conversion rate on big ticket items like cars and boats is small – we don't buy those very often – but the conversion rate on small ticket item like a book or music is much higher.

Assume a 1%-3% conversion rate to begin, and then calculate your *actual* Sales Per Click once you have some monthly data.

Your conversion rate can be improved by optimizing your customer-focused value proposition (see Branding and Customer Focused Value Proposition) and the layout and flow of your website.

Google AdWords | Help | Sign in

Send us feedback!

Tools

Keyword Tool
Traffic Estimator

☆ **Starred (0)**   View

Include terms   ⊕

Exclude terms   ⊕

All Categories

  Apparel
  Computers
                              Show all categories

Match Types
☑ Broad
○ [Exact]
○ "Phrase"

Help

How do I get additional keyword
ideas using categories or related
terms?

What new features do the
updated Keyword and placement
tools offer?

How do I use the keyword tool to
get keyword ideas and traffic
estimates?

Why do search traffic statistics
vary between keyword tools?

Why would I add stars to search
results in the Keyword and
Placement tools?

Help Center

Search help center   Go

Find keywords

Based on one or both of the following:
Word or phrase (one per line):   **Website**

custom netbook

☐ Only show ideas closely related to my search terms ⓘ
⊞ Advanced options   Locations: United States ×   Languages: English ×

  Search

Sign in with your AdWords login information to see the full set of ideas for this search.   About this data ⓘ

Download ▾   View as text ▾   More like these ▾   Sorted by Relevance ▾   Columns

☐	Keyword		Competition	Global Monthly Searches	Local Monthly Searches	Local Search Trends
☑	custom netbook	🔍		1,000	720	
☐	laptop skins	🔍		135,000	74,000	
☐	netbook skins	🔍		9,900	5,400	
☐	laptop computers	🔍		368,000	246,000	
☑	netbooks	🔍		823,000	301,000	
☑	netbook	🔍		6,120,000	1,500,000	
☐	laptops for sale	🔍		246,000	110,000	
☐	notebook computers	🔍		110,000	74,000	
☐	laptop deals	🔍		368,000	201,000	
☐	notebook skins	🔍		9,900	1,900	
☐	mini laptops for sale	🔍		4,400	1,900	
☐	notebook deals	🔍		12,100	8,100	
☐	netbook skin	🔍		9,900	4,400	
☐	mini laptop	🔍		450,000	90,500	
☐	laptop notebook	🔍		246,000	90,500	
☐	computer skins	🔍		12,100	8,100	
☐	notebooks	🔍		1,500,000	301,000	
☐	custom netbook skins	🔍		140	110	
☐	laptop stickers	🔍		22,200	8,100	
☐	buy notebook	🔍		40,500	18,100	

Go to page: 1   Show rows: 50 ▾ |◁ ◁ 1 - 50 of 58 ▷ ▷|

Case Study: How to Calculate Optimal CPC Bids

Martin manufactures custom netbooks and has a unit margin (not including CPC advertising) of $400. He knows this because the retail price of his netbook is $600 and his cost to manufacture and ship is $200.

Given that $400 opportunity, let's figure out how much he should bid for the keywords "custom netbook."

Martin uses Google's Keyword Tool to find 200 keyword ideas for custom netbook. He selects the 50 most relevant keywords, eliminating non-relevant keywords like "netbook skins" and downloads the list into Excel. He copies the list and pastes it into Google's Traffic Estimator Tool.

He inputs a few different estimates of CPC bids and Daily Budgets to maximize the total Estimated Daily Clicks by entering the lowest optimal CPC and the highest Daily Budget he can afford.

Once he's satisfied that he's found the maximum CPC and Daily Budget combination for the most Estimated Daily Clicks, he downloads the Traffic Estimator chart into Excel and calculates the average Estimated Daily Clicks and average Estimated Daily Cost.

Keyword	Global Monthly Searches	Estimated Avg. CPC	Estimated Ad Position	Estimated Daily Clicks	Estimated Daily Cost	Local Monthly Searches
netbook	301,000	$1.16	1.52	95	$111.85	165,000
netbooks	165,000	$1.52	1.52	59	$90.89	110,000
custom netbook	301,000	$2.09	1.57	56	$119.83	201,000
netbooks	49,500	$1.88	1.51	12	$23.80	33,100
netbook	49,500	$2.33	1.55	9	$23.75	33,100
customize netbook	27,100	$1.87	1.52	5	$11.25	22,200
custom netbooks	49,500	$1.55	1.51	1	$2.81	40,500
build your own notebook	4,400	$1.65	1.51	1	$2.85	3,600
custom built netbook	3,600	$1.64	1.5	1	$2.17	2,900
customized netbooks	3,600	$1.89	1.5	1	$2.03	2,900
custom build netbook	5,400	$1.76	1.51	1	$2.82	4,400
customize your netbook	4,400	$1.74	1.26	1	$1.82	3,600
netbook customization	49,500	$1.44	1.5	0	$0.90	40,500
			Average	242	$397	

By dividing the Estimated Daily Cost ($397) by the Estimated Daily Clicks (242), Martin calculates that the average Cost Per Click is $1.64 for his set of keywords.

Now Martin tries to estimate how many sales he will get per click. He knows that if people are searching for custom netbooks and click on his ad, there's a high likelihood they are looking to buy a custom netbook in the near future. He also knows that only a small percentage will purchase a custom netbook from him (he has several competitors) and that an even smaller percentage will purchase a netbook immediately (most of his customers do a lot of clicking and researching before they make a purchase).

Marin estimates that 2% of people clicking on his ad will actually make a purchase that day. He then calculates what his daily number of sales will be based on the daily number of clicks and sales per click. He then estimates his gross margin per day based on the number of sales per day and the gross margin per netbook. Next, he calculates his daily CPC advertising cost based on the cost per click and daily number of clicks.

Assumptions

Gross Margin per Netbook	$400	*from business plan*
Average CPC Advertising Cost	$1.64	*from Traffic Estimator*
Estimated Daily Clicks	242	*from Traffic Estimator*
Estimated Sales per Click	2%	*Martin's guess*

Calculations

Estimated Sales per Day	4.84	*242 x 2% = 4.84*
Gross Margin per Day	$1,936	*4.84 x $400 =$1,936*
Advertising Cost per Day	$397	*242 x $1.64 = $397*
Net Daily Margin	$1,539	*1,936 – 397 = 1,539*

Martin decides that $1.64 CPC is reasonable given his $400 margin and 2% Estimated Sales Per Click. With a 2% conversion rate, he could make $1,539 per day in profit.

To calculate your maximum bid, multiply your Gross Margin by your estimated Sales Per Click. This is your absolute maximum CPC bid.

Maximum CPC Bid = Gross Margin x Conversion Rate

For Martin, $400 multiplied by 2% is $8. He should not bid any more than $8 for a click. At $8 CPC, Martin's Estimated Sales per Day are still $1,936 (he reached the maximum traffic at $1.64 CPC), but now his Advertising Cost per Day is $1,936, so his Net Daily Margin is $0.

Small changes to the CPC bid can have huge effects. This small change from $1.64 to $8 per click resulted in a $1,539 difference in profit per day (from $1,539 in profit to $0 in profit). If Martin bids more than $8 per click, he will lose money.

Small changes to the conversion rate are also significant. If Martin's conversion rate sinks to 0.5%, his profit per day will go down to $87.

Monitor your Number of Monthly Unit Sales and Number of Monthly Clicks closely to determine your actual conversion rate (sales per click).

$$\text{Conversion Rate} = \frac{\text{Number of Monthly Unit Sales}}{\text{Number of Monthly Clicks}}$$

Keep in mind that CPC ads work like any other auction – on any given day the price will go up or down depending on what everyone else is bidding at the moment, so update your calculations regularly as prices change.

Demographic Targeting

Facebook Ads Manager and LinkedIn Direct Ads allow you to target your customer in a whole new way – by demographic.

Keyword advertising is useful for niche products that people might search for, but useless for many new-to-the-world products. People won't search for something they've never heard of.

Advertising to a demographic involves targeting your user by who they are, not what they're searching for. So, if your target customer is a student in their senior year at Stanford, you can use Facebook to target that exact demographic.

If your target customer is a sales manager in the pharmaceutical industry or a VP at Pfizer, you can target that person on LinkedIn using DirectAds. Facebook also allows you to target by company to some degree, but since the platform is more social than professional, they have a limited amount of professional demographic information.

Similar to Google, these ads rates are priced by CPM and CPC. If you are more concerned with raising awareness as opposed to driving traffic to your website or creating a call to action, CPM is usually slightly cheaper and may be a good option for you.

CPC pricing will allow you to track and manage your advertising spending by action, so if your goals are clicks, website traffic, and immediate action, opt for CPC and use the CPC calculations in the case study to determine your maximum bid.

facebook

Profile edit   Friends ▼   Inbox ▼   home account privacy logout

Ads Manager | Pages | Reports | Billing | Help   Create an Ad ▶

Search

Applications   edit
Ad Manager
Mountain Biker
Photos
Groups
Cameron Crazies
fresh BIBLE
+ more

Mountain bike trails rename   Back to Campaign
Ad is ▶ running. ▼

Daily stats for the week of: May 25 ▼

Date	Imp.	Clicks	CTR (%)	Avg. CPC ($)	Avg. CPM ($)	Spent ($)
05/30/2008						
05/29/2008	0	0	0.00	0.00	0.00	0.00
05/28/2008	0	0	0.00	0.00	0.00	0.00
05/27/2008	0	0	0.00	0.00	0.00	0.00
05/26/2008	0	0	0.00	0.00	0.00	0.00
05/25/2008	0	0	0.00	0.00	0.00	0.00

CPC Bid

$ [   ] Update
Changes will be updated within
15 minutes.

Ad Preview

Mountain bike trails

Find the best mountain
bike trails plus read
reviews of the latest gear.

(+ Create a Similar Ad)

Targeting
You are targeting men between
16 and 34 years old in the
United States who like Mountain
Biking.

Social Actions
This ad will display with Social
Actions from:
No Social Action sources

Locations
This ad will display in the:
• News Feed
• Ad Space

Direct Mail

Direct mail is an expensive media that's best for local, targeted consumer advertising or highly targeted business-to-business marketing. On the low end, postcards cost around $0.10 to print and around $0.28 to send. That means that it costs $0.38 per piece, or $380 per thousand pieces, to print and send a postcard via direct mail – that is, if you already own the list.

Direct mail list rental (address lists) is an additional expense and can run around $0.09 per contact. Quotes on specific list rental fees can be found at SRDS.com.

E-mail Marketing List Rental

E-mail list rental companies keep lists of e-mails of millions of consumers and businesses. These companies resell the lists to businesses looking to advertise through e-mail. The majority of these e-mail companies rent the list to the business, meaning that they will send a specified number of e-mails to a specified demographic on your behalf and report the response back to you. At no point will the rental company provide you with any proof of the quality of the list – or let you see the actual list, so it's a bit of a gamble.

Effective e-mail marketing companies are hard to find. The benefit of e-mail marketing is that it's cheap and quantifiable – and is delivered directly to the consumer's inbox. The downside is that the quality of the list is not guaranteed and you may be spending good money to e-mail Nigerian princes about the opening of your new coffee shop.

A better alternative is a targeted lead generation service like Jigsaw, which allows you to individually select the contacts you want to buy. With Jigsaw, you <u>own</u> the list – you don't lease it, so if you plan to send more than one e-mail broadcast (likely), this is a better financial investment.

Most companies are better off creating, growing, and managing their own high-quality list. By owning and controlling the list, you also manage unsubscribers and prevent your brand from being associated with spam and bad marketing practices.

E-mail Newsletters

Depending on the e-mail service, e-mail newsletters can be sent to your list of subscribers for **less than a penny an e-mail** – more precisely, between $0.0067 and $0.01 per e-mail – a deal compared with the $0.28 postage required to send a postcard!

E-mail newsletters are great ways to stay in touch with your customers and engage them regularly with your brand. Make sure that your e-mail template design is a good reflection of your brand, like Etsy's newsletter, "Etsy Success."

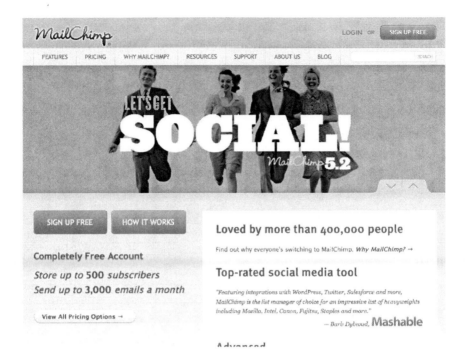

E-mail is among the easiest, cheapest ways to reach your current and potential customers. If you already have a list of customers or a list of people who wouldn't mind getting an e-mail from you about your business, then this will be the starting point for your e-mail list.

Go to Mailchimp.com and sign up for a free account that will allow you to add up to 500 e-mail subscribers before you have to pay to upgrade. Pricing is determined on a sliding scale and depends on the number of subscribers on your list and the number of e-mail newsletters you plan to send each year.

First, create an e-mail list of subscribers. Your list will grow as your business grows, as long as you make a point to collect e-mails at every opportunity.

If your customers are professionals and you want to jumpstart your list, use Jigsaw to find potential customers by company, industry, job title, etc. Each lead costs roughly $1 to purchase, so make sure that your criteria are as targeted as possible.

So, to get started, your e-mail newsletter budget could look something like this:

1. Acquire 5,000 targeted contacts on Jigsaw at $1 per contact = **$5,000**
2. Send 12 newsletters (one each month) to 5,000 subscribers using MailChimp = **$600**

Grand Total = $5,600

Next, design an e-mail template in MailChimp. Your e-mail template should reflect your brand and closely resemble your website – using the same colors, fonts, and imagery, so that your brand image is reinforced every time your customer receives an email. Make sure that your e-mail template is simple and easy to read – and allows the reader to read the highlights of the e-mail "above the fold" – on the top half of the e-mail that shows without scrolling. Not everyone downloads images in their e-mail inbox, so put the important points in a text-only version.

MailChimp's analytics allow you to monitor how many of your emails are opened and how many links are clicked. It automatically handles unsubscribers, new customers, confirmation e-mails, and prevents your e-mails from being tagged as spam.

There are two keys to getting subscribers and keeping them on your list. First, use your e-mails to provide something of value to your customers – like an article that would be interesting or helpful to your customers. If you provide value to your customers, you give them a reason to stay on your list. Avoid needless e-mails. These may do more damage than good – annoying customers and associating your brand with spam.

Along with this value, make sure that you have a call to action. For example, invite them to a VIP sale or send them a coupon. Whatever it may be, make it clear what you want them to do after reading your email.

Time: 1 Hour (import contacts, craft an e-mail campaign)
Cost: Free

Vehicle Lettering

Not all brands – and not all startup CEOs – can pull off a vehicle wrap, but it's an inexpensive way to get your brand in front of thousands of people everyday while you're making deliveries and running errands. A delivery truck in a medium-to-large city will make 16 million impressions in a year.

Any type of household service – landscaping, maid service, in-home nursing, handyman, construction, plumbing, electrical, etc. – should seriously consider a vehicle wrap or magnets.

Vehicle magnets are rectangular magnet signs that attach to the doors of your vehicle and generally only show the company name and telephone number or website. These can run as little as $10 to print, so every vehicle in your fleet should have at least one or two magnets.

Vehicle wraps are much more noticeable – like this RedBull Volkswagen. These wraps can cost anywhere from $2,000 to $5,000 to design and install and are well worth the expense.

Search Engine Optimization (SEO) Basics

Search engine optimization (SEO) simply refers to the act of making your site easy to find on Google, Bing, and other search engines. "Optimized" sites are sites with a high page rank. These are the sites that pop up first when people search for a keyword.

Some company names and keywords have a lot of competition. For instance, "free conference call" is one of the most sought after domain names and keywords online, so gaining page rank in this particular industry is a challenge.

While search engine algorithms are all different and change frequently, the basics are the same across time and across most search engines.

The three main drivers of search engine optimization are
  1. Traffic
  2. Relevance of content (keywords)
  3. Links

Traffic can be direct (someone types your domain name directly into their browser) or come from another source like a search engine. Search engine traffic becomes more and more interesting when you examine the keywords that people are searching for to end up on your site.

Another source of traffic is a referring site like a news article or blog. These sources are extremely important, so make sure to post links to your recent publicity on your site and always include hyperlinks to your site or your full website address (http://www.company.com) in your press releases.

The more people who visit your site, the more relevant you are to search engines, meaning that they will increase your page rank, sending even more people to your site.

Relevance of content is determined by keywords and recency. Older posts and sites that have not been recently updated receive less attention than **recent** posts, so blogs and social media feeds are helpful in keeping your site fresh.

Keywords are extremely important. Most search engines are playing a matching game. When a person types in "Authentic Dutch Wooden Shoes," the search engine will browse the titles and text of all the websites in the world to try to determine which one the user is seeking. The most specific word or set of words will drive most of the searching. In this case, "Dutch" is a pretty specific identifier, as are "Wooden Shoes."

The search engine will try to find the sites that have the most related keywords and list them in order of a combination of relevance, traffic, and links.

Links help drive traffic to your site. The more links pointing to your site, the more traffic you can potentially get from all of those sites. Links are indicators of credibility. Search engines want to present the most credible sites to their users and if other people find your site credible and valuable, they will link to it.

Create links to other sites that your customers would find helpful. If your site is an authority or a resource, users will go to your site more often and spend more time there, again making your site more credible to search engines.

One strategy for link-building is to manufacture your own set of linking sites. With domains costing less than $10/year, strategic domain name acquisition is a cheap and powerful way to establish credibility within search engines. For instance, if you are starting an in-home nursing business in Pittsburgh called "Super Nurses", in addition to acquiring www.supernurses.com, you should also consider acquiring www.pittsburghnurses.com and www.inhomenurses.com – and linking both of those sites to www.supernurses.com. Create content on all three sites and use keywords that are relevant to your offering (like geriatric care, elderly, etc.). Link each site to yours as well as other helpful resource websites about caring for an elderly individual.

Technical Aspects of Search Engine Optimization

Unless you're building your website on your own from scratch in HTML, many of the following tips are more relevant to your website designer than they will be to you, but in order to make you an intelligent consumer of web design services, we will address them anyway.

Mainly, you're going to want to make sure that page titles, descriptions, keyword tags, heading tags, XML sitemap, social media, bookmarking, and Google Analytics are addressed in the scope of your website design. These are the technical building blocks of your website's presence online.

The **title tag** (page title) plays a large role in the indexing of your website and is the first thing a search engine will look at when determining what the particular page is about. It is also the first thing potential visitors will see when looking at your search engine listing.

Most people include the company name here, but an even better approach is to include what product or service you are offering or where you are located. So, for Harry's Landscaping in Buffalo, a good page title would be "Buffalo Landscaping and Snow Removal" instead of just "Harry's Landscaping."

The **description tag** is what users read when your link comes up and what makes them decide whether to click on your link. The description tag should read like a sentence — not a keyword list.

When creating your keyword list, you'll want to think of the specific terms people will type in when searching for your site. Don't go overboard trying to think of every possible combination of keywords, just pick one or two variations per keyword.

To generate keyword recommendations, type your main 2-3 keywords into Google's Keyword Tool and see which keywords get the most traffic.

Heading tags are also very important elements to consider when writing your site copy. Heading tags help web browsers and search engines figure out the main points of your site. Your main page title should use the <h1> tag — this shows what your page is about. Subheadings should use <h2> and <h3> tags.

Search engines use XML sitemaps to index your site. Sitemaps list all of the pages of your site and when the page was last updated – both very important details for search engines.

Don't use Flash for anything important. Search engines do not read Flash – it's treated as an image even though it may have text embedded in the file, so make sure that the important content of your site (keywords, etc.) are not solely embedded in Flash.

Flash is fine for headers and animation, but if you have the core text of your site in Flash, make sure to repeat it in HTML text so that search engines can read it.

Finally, although **social media** is technically not SEO, social media helps your site get noticed. Social media networks include Facebook, Twitter, and LinkedIn, but also social bookmarking sites like ShareThis, Delicious, Digg, Reddit, and StumbleUpon. When your site is mentioned or linked to on these networks, it helps drive traffic to your site.

Get Google Analytics

Google Analytics allows you to track the volume and sources of traffic on your website over time for free, using highly interactive and detailed charts.

In a matter of minutes, you or your web designer can copy and paste a line of HTML code onto your website's source code (just like embedding a YouTube video) and immediately start tracking the people that view and interact with your site.

Not all web analytics engines are created equal, so check your site's traffic numbers on **Compete.com** and **Alexa.com** periodically to get a second opinion on your site traffic.

For a more detailed analysis of what you can do to improve your site's ranking, check out **HubSpot's Website Grader**.

Word-of-Mouth (Viral) Marketing Basics

The difference between word of mouth (or viral) marketing and traditional marketing and PR is how it's tracked.

Traditional marketing and PR is tracked by the number of leads (business cards, email addresses, etc) or press stories the company it generates.

Word of mouth marketing is measured by how many people are exposed to your ideas, or are downloading your eBook – and how often bloggers are writing about you and how you appear in search results. Word-of-mouth marketing is a form of inbound marketing – how many people reach out to you instead of the other way around.

Whole books have been written on word-of-mouth marketing, and the best how-to guide is David Meerman Scott's "World Wide Rave."

Bloggers, Tweeters, and Facebookers control the airways when it comes to most viral, word-of-mouth, and social media marketing, so to get started, make a list of the top bloggers and individuals (Tweeters and Facebookers) who have the most influence in your field. Look for the number of followers, friends, and in the case of bloggers, ranking and web traffic. These individuals are the larger gatekeepers that you eventually want to get your message out to.

However, your message – whether it's a funny YouTube video, informative free eBook, or just a really great blog post – won't necessarily get noticed right away. It has to have momentum first. Word-of-mouth marketing can take a long time to catch on and pay off, so start by building relationships first.

People want to do business with people – not stuffy corporate bureaucracies that don't respond in a human way.

Not every brand can pull off a funny viral YouTube video that makes fun of their company – and not every brand should have a Facebook Fan Page. But for those brands that want to be real, approachable, playful, and engaging, social and viral marketing can be a powerful complement to traditional publicity and advertising.

In order to launch an authentic viral campaign, you're going to have to accept a sad fact: No one cares about your business except for you. People want to connect with real people – not corporations.

To see a great example of an excellently executed viral video campaign, check out BlendTec's "Will it Blend" series on YouTube, which includes classics like "Will It Blend? iPhone" and "Will It Blend? Golf Balls." The campaign is hilarious and will have you asking "Who are these guys?!" – which is exactly the point! "Will It Blend? Glowsticks" has received over 7 million hits. Not bad for a small blender manufacturer.

Create a viral YouTube video. The video should be 3 minutes or less and be either funny or eye opening – anything that will capture the public's attention. Your video should be homemade – not too polished.

A description of your product is not interesting – it's just promotional, so don't try to make a fake advertisement. Save your company information for the end – and include your website or contact information on the last screen of the video.

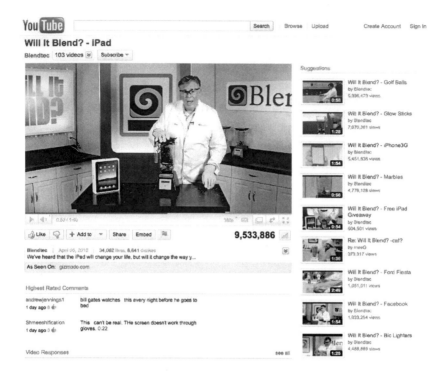

 To get ideas, check out some of the top viewed YouTube videos. Think of shows like Saturday Night Live and America's Funniest Home Videos. YouTube is the user-generated Mecca of comedy and horror. This is what your audience wants! Golf balls in blenders! Break-dancing cats! From hilarious songs and comical bloopers to death-defying feats and animal rampages, viral videos delight and surprise their audience, encouraging them to share the best videos with their friends.

Once your video is uploaded, tell everyone – all your Facebook friends, all your Twitter followers, all your LinkedIn Groups, etc. Make a list of bloggers who might be interested and send them a link.

Participate in social media. Social networks such as Facebook, Twitter, and LinkedIn provide great ways for you to target and connect to customers on a regular basis for free.

facebook Social networks are built for conversation, so steer clear of this media format if you're not ready to talk. Make it easy for people to contact you and create links to all your online content.

The number one rule for Facebook, YouTube, and Twitter is to have fun. People want to interact with people they like, and if you're having fun, they'll have fun too.

Facebook Groups, Facebook Fan Pages, LinkedIn Groups, and Twitter Lists are all useful tools to gain web traffic and raise awareness for your brand. Join and create LinkedIn Groups or Facebook Groups that reach your target audience. These networks can allow you to create hyper-focused groups (Toy and Game Inventors in Charleston), so take advantage of it. Be as focused and targeted as possible.

Consumer-focused brands that want to be approachable should use Facebook and Twitter to reach out to their fans and followers.

If you are **marketing to businesses** and you are trying to establish "expert" status, **LinkedIn** use LinkedIn and Twitter to promote your message. Create a regular daily or weekly schedule to create Tweets and LinkedIn posts. Link to relevant articles in your industry that you find interesting and that would be helpful to your customers. By being helpful and providing valuable information, customers will turn to you when they need you.

Become an online **thought leader**. Twitter is one of the best platforms for professional thought leadership, allowing you to publish or link to helpful articles – all in 140 characters. Tech-savvy professionals appreciate Twitter's ultra-short "Readers Digest Version" of user-generated news. Because Twitter is a social network, news is being generated and talked about 24-7, so you have plenty of opportunity to pass along helpful information and express your opinion.

Probably the best way to establish your expertise is to publish an eBook and allow people to download it for free. Make sure to promote your eBook in the press and let bloggers know about it. eBooks are great conversation pieces for bloggers because they create value for their readers.

Make it easy for people to share your content with sharing buttons like ShareThis. These buttons allow users to bookmark and share links easily with their Facebook friends, Twitter followers, and LinkedIn contacts at the touch of a button, driving traffic to your site. ShareThis is free and is a clean, one-button solution for all social media and bookmarking sites.

Customer Relationship Management (CRM)

Selling to individual customers in person or via phone can be challenging and time consuming. These customer relationships are rich in details, dates, deadlines, follow up, responses, and feedback. Managing all these details can be tough for any startup or large business and Customer Relationship Management (CRM) software can help.

Salesforce.com is an industry leading CRM software that's priced for businesses of all sizes. Salesforce.com allows you to create sales goals, monitor the status of proposals, and keep track of all your contact with customers.

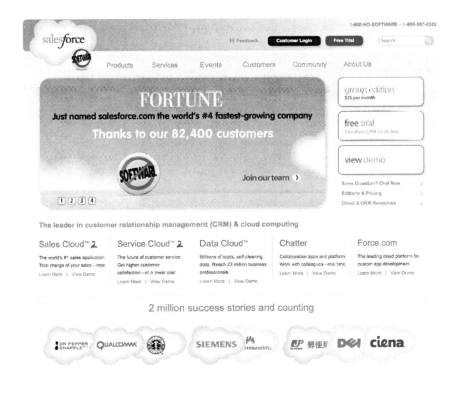

The software is easily scalable, allowing you to add new sales reps to your company and quickly get them up to speed on sales. The software also helps coordinate and manage sales teams, getting everyone on the same page with a dashboard view of sales goals and current performance.

The software also integrates easily into Google Apps, Intuit QuickBooks accounting software, and other major business software. Subscriptions start at $5 per month.

Getting Government Contracts

The U.S. government is the largest single purchasing organization in the world. Selling to the government can be very lucrative, but registering and bidding can be time consuming. Before you spend any time registering for government contracts, make sure that the government is looking to buy services or products like yours.

Central Contractor Registration

| CCR Home | CCR Search | Federal Agency Registration | News | Release Notes | Request Data Access | Help |
| Contractors | Grantees | International Registrants | Small Businesses | Security Notes | | 600,147 Active Registrants |

Quick Links

Dynamic Small Business Search

ORCA

SBA

Request DUNS Number

Federal Business Opportunities

Welcome to Central Contractor Registration (CCR)

Central Contractor Registration (CCR) is the primary registrant database for the U.S. Federal Government. CCR collects, validates, stores and disseminates data in support of agency acquisition missions. Learn more about CCR Policy and Background.

Log in to CCR

User ID: [   ] [Log In]
Password: [   ]

Forgot User ID   **Forgot Password**

Create New Registration

[Start New Registration]
What You Need to Register
International Registrants
Note: New registrations usually take **3-5** business days to process once completed by the vendor.

Top Frequently Asked Questions

How do I register in CCR?
Follow these steps: Step 1: Access the CCR...

What are my yearly renewal requirements? How do I keep my record active?
You must renew and revalidate your registration...

How are CAGE Codes assigned?
Background: The Commercial And Government Entity...

I am updating and renewing my CCR record and noticed that the D&B information provided requires changing. How can I update this data?
Update your D&B information on the D&B...

What is an MPIN? Where can I locate or assign my MPIN?
A Marketing Partner ID Number (MPIN) is a...

View All FAQs

CCR News and Announcements

07/28/2010 CCR Release 4.10.3 Implemented
07/07/2010 CCR Release 4.10.2.1 Implemented
06/23/2010 Disaster Response Contractors
06/23/2010 SIC Codes will be going away in CCR

CCR Active Registrations Over Time

Date	Contracts	Grants	Contracts/Grants
11/27/2010	329,565	76,954	189,134
11/20/2010	329,386	75,727	188,886
11/13/2010	330,352	75,794	189,405

Women-owned and Minority-owned Businesses

Women-owned and minority-owned businesses benefit from special programs called Supplier Diversity Programs.

Large corporations and local, state, and federal governments use supplier Diversity Programs to create opportunities for disadvantaged groups.

Some programs require certifications from the SBA or a third-party organization like NAWBO or WEBNC. Third-party certifications can cost as much as $500. Certification is not always required, so double check with the government agency or corporation before you pay to be certified.

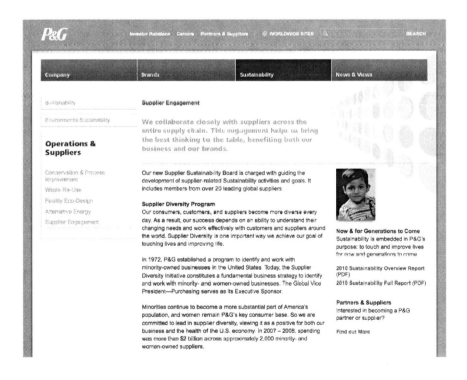

8   Managing Administrative Details

"Never neglect details. When everyone's mind is dulled or distracted, the leader must be doubly vigilant."

   -    *Colin Powell*

Setting up new business operations, especially IT, phones, and accounting, can be expensive and time consuming. In this chapter, we'll explore simple ways to save money and save time by doing it yourself online.

First, we'll cover business cards and letterhead. Then we'll show you how to create your own website, set up e-mail, back up your data, and launch an online store. We'll also show you some simple tools for project management.

Finally, we'll explore inexpensive ways to manage your accounting and taxes effectively.

Printing Business Cards and Letterhead

Once you've had business cards and letterhead professionally designed, there are several options for professional printing, depending on your budget, desired quality, and timeline.

You can get business cards and letterhead printed inside of 24 hours through Kinko's and local printers, or within a week if you order online. Uploading your designs takes minutes.

Cheap: VistaPrint and Overnight Prints are the cheapest options for printing online. Both run frequent specials like "Your first 200 business cards free" or "25% off for first time customers," so make sure to check for online promo codes on RetailMeNot.com.

http://www.vistaprint.com
http://www.overnightprints.com

Better & Best: Moo and 4by6 are higher quality online printers and slightly more expensive than VistaPrint and Overnight Prints. These printers use fine-quality paper and finishes.

4by6 offers an excellent free paper sampler (satin, recycled, etc.) so that you can touch and feel the paper before placing an order.

http://www.moo.com
http://www.4by6

Fast: Fedex Kinko's Print Online service allows you to upload your designs and documents online and pick them up the same day from your nearest FedEx Kinko's location:

http://fedex.com/us/office/copyprint/online/index.html

Setting up a Website

Not all businesses need websites, but most need at the very least a simple, tasteful splash page. A splash page gives you a presence on the web and is inexpensive to launch.

Businesses such as quick-service restaurants and other retail businesses can sometimes get away without a website at first and start with a listing on Google Places. This listing allows people searching for your address or phone number online to find you quickly and easily.

Choosing the right domain name

A domain name is a web address (ex. www.company.com). Finding the right domain name is critical for you company's credibility. Billions of domain names have already been purchased by others so check if the domain you want is still available, by visiting GoDaddy.com. Type in your business name and it will instantly show you whether the .com, .net, and .org of that name is still available.

Here are some tips for creating effective domain names:
- Don't include hyphens (-) or underscores (_) in your domain name
- Don't include numbers or roman numerals
- Keep it short. The shorter, the more memorable and the more traffic and sales you'll get from your website. Acme.com is far better than acmeproductsandservices.com.
- Keep it related to your business. If it's not your exact business name, it should be as close as possible.

Your web address is a crucial point of contact for potential customers. Don't rush to choose something without thought. Time spent here will pay off for the lifetime of your business.

Option 1: Hire a web designer and buy your domain and web hosting from GoDaddy

If you have trouble navigating the Internet as it is, this is probably the best option for you. Hiring a designer also guarantees that the site you launch will look completely professional and launch on time. Simple websites that don't involve custom software applications can be designed for $1,000-$5,000.

To find a local web designer or developer, go to Behance.net, search your city, and sort by creative field (web designer). Crowdspring is also another great option for uncoded designs.

If you use Crowdspring, you'll have to hire a web developer to implement the design.

GoDaddy is the best domain name and web hosting option for most small businesses. They offer monthly plans starting at $7.99/month.

To get started, go to GoDaddy.com and sign up for a one-year or longer account. Choosing longer plans will give you larger monthly discounts. Within a few hours, you should receive information about your account and you are ready to go live on the web. Need help? GoDaddy has a world-class support team available 24/7.

Time: 30 minutes
Cost: $9.99/month + $10.69/yr to register your domain

Option 2: Design (and host) your own on Squarespace

Setting up a website often seems like a daunting task for entrepreneurs, but it doesn't have to be.

Squarespace offers do-it-yourself design and hosting all in one place. Setting up a site is simple:
1. Create an account
2. Snap your website together like bricks
3. Choose an overall design and color scheme
4. Type in your content
5. Connect your domain name URL

Squarespace is perfect for any business that can't afford to hire a designer or that doesn't need a lot of design. In these cases, Squarespace can provide you with a professional-looking website at a minimal cost.

Squarespace hosts your files for your website but doesn't handle e-mail accounts. If you choose Squarespace, buy your domain name from GoDaddy – it's easier to setup e-mail later. Be sure to purchase just the domain name from GoDaddy – hosting is provided by Squarespace. After you buy a domain name from GoDaddy, visit Squarespace's help section to find easy step-by-step instructions on how to connect it with Squarespace. http://manual.squarespace.com/domain-setup/domain-mapping-with-godaddy-new-interface.html

Time: 3-5 Hours to enter content
Cost: $14/month + $10.69/yr for a domain from GoDaddy

Google Apps

By far, the best suite of online tools for businesses is Google Apps. Google Apps includes services like email, calendars, phone lines, voicemail, and project management tools. All of these tools are free and easy to set up.

- **Gmail** - free web email (with your domain name – you@company.com)
- **Google Voice** - free business line and voicemail
- **Google Calendar** - free online calendar
- **Google Docs** - free online project management and collaboration tools

Because Google Apps is cloud-hosted (online, not on your desktop computer), you can access it from anywhere – and it's always backed up.

To start, create a Google account, also known as a personal Gmail account (you@gmail.com) at www.gmail.com.

Take a moment to get comfortable with the functionality of Gmail, Google Calendar, and Google Docs, before setting up Google Apps for your company.

Set up a Phone Line & Voicemail

Next, sign up for a Google Voice account (www.google.com/voice), request a phone number, and forward it to your phone. Request a phone number with your local area code to avoid long distance charges to your local customers. Voicemails are automatically transcribed and forwarded to your email.

Time: 10 minutes
Cost: Free

Set up E-mail with Google Apps

Now that you have purchased a domain name, you are ready to set up your business e-mail accounts (you@company.com). With Gmail (Google mail), your mail is hosted in the cloud on Google's servers, meaning that it's accessible from anywhere and always backed up. Gmail also has a free mobile mail app for BlackBerry, iPhone, and Android, making it a great choice for startups.

GoDaddy provides their own options for creating e-mail, but use the free version of Google Apps. Google Apps is backed by Google servers and Gmail's user interface – and has important spam blocking features. Here's how to set up Google Apps for e-mail for your company:

1. Go to Google and sign up for an account
2. Follow the step-by-step instructions and enter your domain name information
3. If you hosted your domain with GoDaddy, login to GoDaddy's Gmail configurator and it will configure your mail for you: https://www.godaddy.com/gdshop/google/gmail_login.asp
4. Add e-mail accounts for each employee and each department of your company (sales, support, etc.).
5. Your e-mail accounts are now set up and ready to go. You can access them at mail.*company*.com, where *company* is your company's domain name.

Time: 10-30 minutes to set up Google Apps for your e-mail
Cost: Free

Project Management with Google Docs

Collaborating on a large project with many people? Whether you're in the same room with your project partner(s) or oceans apart, Google Docs is a great way to collaborate on Microsoft Word, Excel, and PowerPoint documents together. An unlimited number of people can edit a single document simultaneously, creating true real-time collaboration.

With Google Docs, you can create and share your work online and access your documents from anywhere. Manage documents, spreadsheets, presentations, surveys, and more all in one easy platform. You will need a Google Gmail or Google Apps account in order to own any of the documents, but collaborators you invite via e-mail (granting access) will not need a Google account.

Time: 1 minute to set up — just click on Documents
Cost: Free

Project Management with Basecamp

If you have a project that involves  many large files and multiple contributors, Basecamp can help keep everyone organized and on schedule. Basecamp is a project management and collaboration platform that allows you to create project rooms where people can share files, send messages, and create deadlines.

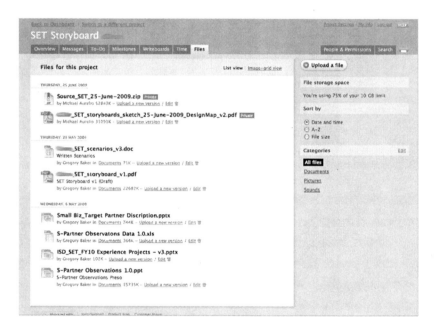

Your files are hosted in the cloud, so you can access them securely from anywhere. Communication is streamlined with a message board and file sharing. Your calendar is integrated with your to-do list so you always know what's going on and what's coming up.

Plans range from $24 per month for 15 projects (5GB of storage and unlimited users) to $149 per month for an unlimited number of projects (75 GB of storage, unlimited number of users) and time-tracking capability.

Back up Your Files

As an entrepreneur out on your own, chances are that there's no full-time IT pro down the hall to help you recover your files if your computer crashes, so money spent on backup is money well spent.

You can back up your files locally, using a $100 desktop external hard drive (like Western Digital's 2 TB backup drive) or you can back up your files online in the cloud with a service like Mozy or Mac's MobileMe iDisk. Mozy starts at around $5/month.

The risk of backing up your files locally is that if your computer is physically in danger of electrical surge, flood, fire, etc. – your backup drive that's sitting right next to it is in the same danger. Backing up remotely in the cloud ensures that your data is safe even if your office is not.

Creating an Online Store

There are three great options for creating your own online store, depending on how many products you want to sell and how much you want to spend on design:

1. Google Checkout
2. GoDaddy Quick Cart
3. Shopify

Google checkout store gadget
labs

The Google Checkout store gadget allows you to quickly and easily create an online store using a Google Docs spreadsheet. No complicated coding or technical tasks are required. You can get your first online store up-and-running in under five minutes.

1. Sign up for Google Checkout

Create Online Store Now

2. List products in a spreadsheet

Manage inventory in Google Docs.

3. Embed the gadget anywhere

Use with Blogger, Google Sites, and websites.

Google Checkout Store Gadget is the fastest and cheapest option for launching a store with a few products. There's no monthly fee and no percentage of sales – just a 2.9% credit card transaction fee. Google Checkout is the primary competitor to PayPal. It allows you to safely accept credit card payments over the web without buying security certificates. The transaction fees are the same as PayPal's (and other credit card processing providers): 2.9% + $0.30 per transaction.

To create a store, simply sign up for a Google Checkout account. Then, create a Google Docs spreadsheet of the products you want to sell. Google will create an embed code for your store widget, which you can copy and paste into any website or blog.

GoDaddy Quick Shopping Cart is fast, reasonably priced, and has the most bells and whistles. For a large online store, this is your best option. There's a low monthly fee of $9.99 and no percentage of sales.

GoDaddy Quick Cart integrates with Intuit's Merchant Account for Webstores, meaning that you'll spend less on credit card transaction fees and be able to track your inventory and sales seamlessly in QuickBooks.

Shopify is the most expensive of the three options, but offers the best designs. If you're a high-end online retailer, this may be your best option. Plans start at $24.99 and 2% of sales. Credit-card processing fees are an additional 2%-3%.

Online Transactions with Credit Cards

There are many providers of online credit card processing, but the four best and most commonly used providers are:

1. PayPal
2. Authorize.net
3. Google Checkout
4. Intuit Merchant Account for Webstores

Paypal

Depending on what you're selling, offering PayPal as an option at checkout is generally a good idea. Frequent online shoppers find the one-button checkout convenient – and the easier you can make the shopping experience for them, the better your online sales will be.

With PayPal, there are no monthly fees or setup fees.

Monthly sales	Transaction Fees	Examples
$0 to $3,000	2.9% + $0.30	$3.20 fee on a $100 sale
$3,000 to $10,000	2.5% + $0.30	$2.80 fee on a $100 sale
$10,000+	2.2% + $0.30	$2.50 fee on a $100 sale

Authorize.net

Authorize.net is widely used by web developers for web stores and has a low monthly fee ($9.95/mo). Transaction fees range from 2% to 3%.

Google Checkout

With Google Checkout, there are no monthly, setup, or gateway service fees. Similar to PayPal, your transaction processing rates are determined by your sales volume during the prior month.

Monthly Sales	Transaction Fees
Less than $3,000	2.9% + $0.30
$3,000 - $9,999.99	2.5% + $0.30
$10,000 - $99,999.99	2.2% + $0.30
$100,000 or more	1.9% + $0.30

Intuit Merchant Account for Web Stores

If you're going to take credit card information securely and directly on your site, the Inuit Merchant Account for Web Stores is your best option. Your webstore will be directly integrated with your QuickBooks Online accounting software, saving you time and money, reducing errors and eliminating double data entry.

Intuit has lower transaction fees and authorization fees, but charges $19.95 monthly.

Rates
- Transaction fee: 2.44%
- Per-authorization fee $0.27
- Monthly service $19.95
- Monthly Minimum fee $0-$20 (based on monthly processing volume)
- One-time set-up fee $59.95

Accounting

QuickBooks Online Simple Start
Cost: $12.95/mo

For business accounting and tax software, the industry standard is Intuit QuickBooks and Intuit TurboTax. Intuit is focused on helping small businesses understand and manage their own accounting and taxes. Their software is updated yearly to comply with new IRS tax laws and new GAAP (Generally Accepted Accounting Practices) accounting rules, so you'll always be up to date and in compliance with new laws.

Intuit's online version of QuickBooks is the simplest and easiest to use. It's also the **most convenient and cost-effective option** for startups. The online version, which starts at $12.95/mo, is $25 cheaper than the desktop CD-ROM, which retails for $180.

QuickBooks Online Simple start is a **complete accounting solution** for businesses of all sizes. Create estimates, send invoices, and manage your store's inventory, your employees' time cards and payroll, your sales and customer data. You can also print reports like your income statement, balance sheet, and cash flow statement quickly and easily.

QuickBooks makes tracking sales and expenses, printing reports, and monitoring your company's performance easy. The company snapshot gives you a big picture view of performance in a single easy-to-understand dashboard – showing what you're making, what you're spending, and how you're doing this year compared with last year.

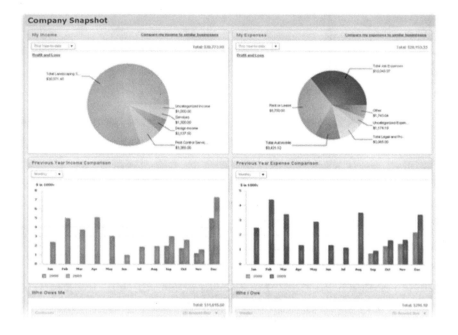

The online version is cloud-hosted and completely mobile. It allows you to log in to your books from anywhere, collaborate remotely with your partners or accountant, and view your books on any iPhone, BlackBerry, or Android. This mobile capability makes it easy to manage payables, receivables, bank balances, and customer contact information.

Benefits of Going Online – and Mobile

With QuickBooks Online, you have the freedom to work from the office, the home, or the road — you're not bound to a single physical location. You can print off an invoice from a client's office, do a quick job on the weekend without having to drive to the office, or check in while traveling.

Having your books online also makes it easy for your accountant to log in securely and close your books at the end of the year or prepare your taxes.

Intuit has world-class **customer service** and a large online community that can guide you through any tough accounting questions.

To ensure your data's **security** over the Internet, QuickBooks Online uses the same data-encryption technology as leading banks. QuickBooks Online is also a VeriSign Secured product. QuickBooks stores your data on the same servers that TurboTax uses to process millions of tax returns each year. These servers are protected by firewall software, intrusion detection software and hardware, and security systems and personnel. They also back up your data daily to help protect you against anything that might happen to your computer.

Keeping track of **customers**, invoices, contact information, and estimates is easy – it's all on one screen. Creating professional-looking **invoices** takes minutes. Print and mail invoices – or e-mail them directly from QuickBooks. Keep track of who owes you money and whether you've been paid.

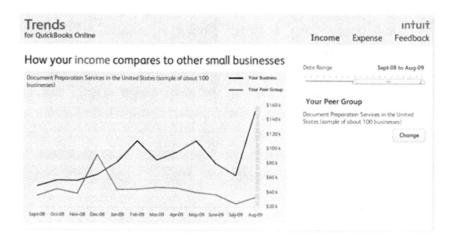

QuickBooks also generates **industry reports** to show you how your company is doing compared with others. Check out reports on what (anonymous) companies in your general industry are spending on advertising or materials – and what they're making in revenue.

QuickBooks Online allows you to accept, authorize, and process **credit card transactions** directly from QuickBooks. Payment information is automatically updated in QuickBooks Online so **you never have to enter data twice.** Grow your business, get paid faster and save money on hardware and phone lines for credit card terminals. Merchant fees are 2.44% (compared with 2.5%-3%

industry average) and you don't need to purchase any additional hardware or software.

Save time entering your bank balances by connecting Quickbooks Online with your bank accounts and credit cards, eliminating the need to **reconcile your books** with your accounts. QuickBooks downloads updates automatically and compares bank balances to book balances.

If you carry **inventory**, you can use QuickBooks to help you manage and track orders, inventory, and sales. QuickBooks tracks which items are in inventory, how much of them you've sold and how much you have on hand, improving inventory counts and reducing lost sales due to out-of-stock items.

Your inventory data is automatically updated behind-the-scenes, keeping your financial statements accurate and up-to-date. This helps you stay IRS–compliant when purchasing and selling items. QuickBooks Online uses the first-in, first-out (FIFO) method, which is compliant with generally accepted accounting principles (GAAP) and accepted by the IRS.

If you charge your clients based on hours – or if you have employees, QuickBooks **Time Tracking** helps you keep track of time so that you can bill customers for that time and pay employees for the hours worked. This feature is great for tracking your labor costs by job – and ultimately, the true profit of each job.

With Time Tracking, you can allow an unlimited number of employees to have "time-entry" access. Employees and contractors can enter time from any Internet connection. To keep your finances protected, you can give these users "time-entry only" access and then choose whether to restrict them from seeing their billing rate. Charges for their time can appear on the client or customer invoice. For employees, the time they have entered flows right into payroll where you can review the hours and print paychecks.

Payroll and direct deposit are easy to run with QuickBooks. Paycheck amounts are calculated instantly based on employee time sheets or salaries. Once you approve the paychecks, you can pay employees with free direct deposit, or print checks and stubs on your own printer.

QuickBooks helps you manage federal and state **payroll taxes**. These taxes are automatically calculated for you — just click to pay and file, or print completed forms on your printer. QuickBooks Online Payroll lets you keep your payroll tax money until it's due. Documents for quarterly and year-end tax filings (like W-2s) are easy to prepare, but if you have trouble, take advantage of the live support available by phone, chat, and e-mail.

QuickBooks Online helps you know where your business stands by tracking the profitability of your business locations. You can track accounting data from **different locations, stores, territories, or divisions** of the same company. By assigning a location to each transaction, you can report profitability and sales by location.

Create a professional-looking **estimate** when you want to give your customer a quote, bid, or proposal for work you plan to do. The estimate form looks very much like an invoice, but its purpose is to help you begin negotiations with your customer. Once the work is done and you're ready to bill your customer, you can move the estimated charges onto an invoice for billing, saving time by eliminating the need to retype information.

Because Intuit's products are the industry standard, QuickBooks **integrates easily with other services like Salesforce.com** and Microsoft. Integrate your Salesforce CRM and sales platform directly with your QuickBooks Online accounting software to reduce redundant data entry, save time, improve reporting and collections, and eliminate duplicates and data errors.

Taxes

TurboTax for Entrepreneurs

If you are making less than $250,000 in revenue and have fewer than five employees, try filing your taxes yourself with Intuit's TurboTax. TurboTax guides you through your taxes step by step, so that your personal and business deductions are maximized and your calculations are accurate.

TurboTax offers two kinds products for startups depending on the legal structure of your company – LLC, C-Corp, etc.

TurboTax *Home & Business* is for sole-proprietors, consultants, 1099 contractors, or single-member LLCs. If your business is organizes as one of these legal structures, the IRS allows you to file your personal and business taxes in one filing. TurboTax Home & Business takes care of your business and personal filings in one sitting.

TurboTax *Business* is for S Corps, C Corps, partnerships, and multi-member LLCs. TurboTax Business covers your federal business tax return for:
- Multi-Member LLCs (Form 1065)
- Partnerships (Form 1065)
- S Corporations (Form 1120S)
- C Corporations (Form 1120)
- Estates and Trusts (Form 1041)

The IRS requires that business taxes for S Corps, C Corps, partnerships, and multi-member LLCs be filed separately from personal taxes. After you do your business taxes with TurboTax Business, you'll need to do your personal taxes. Depending on how complex your personal taxes are, use software like TurboTax Deluxe.

	Turbo Tax Home & Business	Turbo Tax Business
Consultants	✓	
1099 Contractors	✓	
Sole proprietors	✓	
Single-member LLC	✓	
S-Corp		✓
C-Corp		✓
Partnership		✓
Multi-member LLC		✓

TurboTax is written in plain English, so even if you're not savvy about taxes and accounting, you don't have to worry. TurboTax asks you simple questions, such as "Did you start a business this year?" and determines for you which forms will be required – and fills them out for you in the background.

Guidance and answers to commonly asked tax questions are available on every screen as you walk through the questions. You can stop and save your answers at any time – and work at your own pace.

TurboTax is great at finding deductions. TurboTax comes with **extra guidance for new businesses** and advice about the startup deductions new businesses can take. See which expenses you can deduct for your vehicle, supplies, utilities, home office expenses, and more, so that you get every business deduction you deserve. TurboTax will automatically generate a list of **industry-specific deductions** and tax write-offs for your industry to help you spot commonly overlooked deductions.

They also simplify calculations and help you make important tax treatment decisions regarding vehicle deductions (actual expenses vs. mileage rate), asset depreciation (straight-line vs. accelerated), and property. The software is also set up to handle every imaginable taxable event – including stocks and investments, donations, medical expenses, rental income, and changes in family situations.

TurboTax takes minutes to set up. Simply import your tax information from last year (for example from TurboTax, TaxACT, H&R Block and other major tax services) or a PDF of last year's return. You can also import your financial data from QuickBooks, Quicken, or Microsoft Money and automatically download W-2 and 1099 info from over 100,000 participating large employers and large financial institutions.

TurboTax stands by its calculations. Before you file, the software completes thousands of **error checks** on your tax return to help make sure that it is accurate and that you avoid triggering an audit. If you should get hit with an IRS or state penalty due to a TurboTax calculation error, they'll pay the penalty.

TurboTax also calculates your **audit risk**. It monitors your tax return for common audit triggers and shows whether your risk is high or low. If your risk is high, TurboTax provides tips to help you reduce your chance of an audit. Need help? Get **live support** and answers online from TurboTax experts and other users in the Live Community.

When you're finished, you can submit your taxes online directly to the IRS and your state tax bureau from TurboTax and have your **refund** paid via direct deposit.

9   **Make it Legal**

I busted a mirror and got seven years bad luck, but my lawyer thinks he can get me five.
- Stephen Wright

Business law is mostly focused on limiting risk.

Starting a business requires that you have at least a rudimentary understanding of business law. The law has many facets – and we won't tackle all of them in this chapter, but we will cover the main topics that concern startups: incorporation, employment law, taxes, raising capital, intellectual property, contracts, real estate, and product liability.

We'll also examine strategies to limit your risk through the structure of your company (sole proprietor vs. LLC), agreements such as non-disclosures and non-competes, lease terms, investment structures such as convertible notes, intellectual property protection such as copyrights, trademarks, trade secrets, and patents, and business insurance.

Probably the most important law for business owners to be aware of is Murphy's Law: Anything that could go wrong likely will. Your first strategy should be to work with people you trust. Contracts and agreements can't always protect you – and they are expensive to enforce. You're going to be working with a lot of new people in your startup, so don't rush into important relationships with potential employees or contractors and make sure to get good recommendations and references for people you intend to do business with.

Even when you're certain that you can trust someone, get everything in writing. Contracts help set expectations and keep everyone on the same page.

Creating a Legal Entity

Depending on the type of business you start, you may need to form a legal entity such as a corporation or a limited liability company. Not all types of businesses are required to file forms or register with the IRS in order to start doing business.

Choosing the Right Structure

There is no universally "right" structure for all businesses, but these five questions will help you decide what structure is right for you:

1. Is there a great risk of liability associated with your specific business?
2. Will you have investors as shareholders in your company?
3. Do you want to maintain control of the company if you have investors involved?
4. Do you anticipate losses in the early years that can be taken as tax benefits?
5. Do you want to avoid double taxation?

A **sole proprietorship** is appropriate for artists, consultants, and professionals starting out without employees who are working out of their home. Without a physical space where customers or employees might get hurt, a product that might harm someone, or employees who could be injured on the job, the potential liability of these businesses is much less than restaurant, retail, product, and manufacturing companies.

This structure does not require any filings or formal documentation. You can start calling yourself a sole proprietorship today. When you pay your taxes, you'll report the profits and losses of your business on Schedule C.

A **general partnership** is appropriate if you have one or more partners in your business and your potential liability is low (as opposed to restaurant, retail, product, and manufacturing companies). No formal filings are required, but you should create a partnership agreement, which details each partner's responsibilities and their percentage ownership. When you file your taxes, you will file a Return of Partnership Income form.

A **limited partnership** has two components: general and limited. Limited partners are investors who have no control over the business, but share in the profits and losses based on their investment. General partners run the business and are liable for the debts and agreements made on behalf of the company.

A **limited liability company (LLC)** combines the liability protection of a corporation with the simplicity and tax benefits of a sole proprietorship, making it a favorite for small business owners. You can file for an LLC yourself just by registering two legal documents with your state: your Articles of Organization and an Operating Agreement.

LLCs benefit from pass-through tax treatment, meaning that the income of the business (and entrepreneur) is only taxed once – at the entrepreneur's personal income tax rate.

Raising capital is possible with LLCs through the sale of membership interests. Angel investors are able to invest in LLCs, but if the company plans to raise capital from venture capital funds or a public offering, it will have to convert to a C Corporation first.

A **C Corporation** is appropriate for companies that have big plans for growth (in terms of revenue and employees) and plan to raise equity from venture capital funds or public offerings.

Sometimes it doesn't make sense to start out as a C Corp. In the first few years of a startup, the business has losses – which create tax benefits. In the case of a C Corp, these losses cannot pass through to the owners. C Corps are taxed first at the corporate level and then again at the shareholder (entrepreneur/ owner/ investor) level – also known as double taxation.

C Corps require annual reports, formal board meetings and shareholder meetings, and meeting minutes. These stringent requirements mean that attorneys and accountants have to be involved. Because of the significant reporting requirements, this structure is not recommended for most single-person startups initially for the first few years.

An **S corporation** has the limited liability of a corporation with the pass-through tax treatment of a sole proprietorship. On the downside, it requires the same reporting requirements as a C Corporation. LLCs have the same benefits as S Corps without the reporting requirements and are easier to maintain. LLCs are favored over S Corps by most startups.

Venture capital funds prefer C Corps because they do not want to see pass-through income. Most large corporations are incorporated in Delaware because of its highly developed corporate legal system.

For entrepreneurs without VC funding, limited liability companies are the preferred choice since losses in the first few years can pass-through for personal tax deductions. Delaware now allows an easy conversion from an LLC to a C Corp.

There are several other special business structures that are not discussed in this book: *Professional Corporations, Limited Liability Partnerships,* and *Professional Limited Liability Companies.*

These structures are mostly for professional service firms such as accounting firms and law firms where there are multiple partners. Most of these entities do not apply to startup companies, but if you are forming a professional services partnership, you should investigate these structures before making a decision.

Entity type	What is it	Limited Liability	Taxation
Sole Proprietorship	Business owned by one person. It is not incorporated or an LLC.	No	**Pass-through.** Owner reports profit or loss on personal tax return.
General Partnership (GP)	Business owned by more than one person where all the partners are active in the management of the business.	No	**Pass-through.** Owner reports profit or loss on personal tax return.
Limited Partnership (LP)	LPs are investors that invest in General Partnerships. Limited partners do not participate in the management of the business.	Yes	**Pass-through.** Owner reports profit or loss on personal tax return. Can only deduct passive losses against passive income.
Limited Liability Company (LLC)	One or more than one person (members). Provides the liability protection of a corporation with the simplicity and tax benefits of a sole proprietorship. Best for startups in the first few years (during losses and before VC funding & IPO).	Yes	**Pass-through.** Owner reports profit or loss on personal tax return. Can elect to be taxed like a sole proprietor or a corporation. Can distribute profits and losses disproportionate to ownership.
C Corp	A legal entity, separate from its owners. Can have an unlimited number of shareholders. Best for startups raising VC funding or going public (IPO).	Yes	**Double taxation.** Income taxed at corporate and personal (shareholder) level.
S Corp	A type of corporation that allows for pass-through taxation instead of double taxation. S Corps are less popular since the introduction of the LLC.	Yes	**Pass-through.** Owner reports profit or loss on personal tax return. Profits and losses must be distributed according to ownership.

Formation	Maintenance	Advantages	Disadvantages
Simplest. No legal forms or cost to establish a Sole Proprietorship.	None	Simple and inexpensive to create and manage.	Owners are personally liable for business liabilities.
Simple. No legal forms required, but a Partnership Agreement is recommended.	None	Simple and inexpensive to create and manage.	Owners are personally liable for business liabilities.
Simple. No legal forms required, but a Partnership Agreement is recommended.	None	Simple and inexpensive to create and manage.	If LPs participate in the management of the business, they become personally liable.
Minimal filings and fees. LLCs must file Articles of Organization with their state. **Ability to raise capital** through the sale of member interests (i.e., Angel Investors).	**Minimal** maintenance required compared to C Corps and S Corps. Some annual fees may be required.	Most flexible & inexpensive. Liability protection and pass-through tax treatment. No tax penalty for converting to a C Corp.	Slightly more expensive than a sole proprietorship.
Significant. Bylaws and registration with Secretary of State required. Registration may be required If stock is sold. Unlimited number of shareholders.	**Significant.** Formal board and shareholder meetings with meeting minutes required. Annual state reports.	**Limited liability. Ability to raise capital** through sale of stock (VC or IPO). Employee stock options possible.	Double taxation. Significant legal maintenance (meetings, minutes, annual reports).
Significant. More formality and record keeping required than with an LLC, which offers similar advantages. No more than 100 shareholders.	**Significant.** Formal board and shareholder meetings with meeting minutes required. Annual state reports.	Limited liability. No double taxation.	Significant legal maintenance. Eligibility req's. No ability to go public (must be converted to C Corp). Taxed when converted to C Corp.

Option 1: Talk to an attorney

This is the safest bet. A corporate attorney might charge $500-$2,000 to guide you through the right structure, create the necessary documents, and register your company. The steps to actually register a company are pretty simple (everything is mostly online with the IRS and the state's secretary of state) and the required documents (for example, Bylaws or Operating Agreements or Articles of Incorporation) are boilerplate templates.

The benefits to engaging a lawyer now are getting one-on-one advice and beginning what will likely be a long-term relationship. People need dentists just as often as companies need lawyers – and having someone who knows your company inside out from the start is a bonus.

Option 2: File online with MyCorporation.com

MyCorporation
An Intuit Company

You can save time and money by filing online with MyCorporation.com. The site offers several tutorials and a step-by-step "Help Me Choose" wizard that will help you select a business structure. Once you've selected the type of entity you want to create, they will generate the necessary documents and send them to you.

MyCorporation will also register your company with your state and file with the IRS to get a Federal Tax ID (also known as EIN – Employer Identification Number) for you.

Cost: $100-$150
Time: 30 minutes

Registering with federal, state, and local authorities

1. Choose a business structure.

2. Register Your Business Name. Your business' legal name is required on all government forms and applications, including your application for employer tax IDs, licenses and permits. *http://business.gov/register/business-name/dba.html*

3. Obtain an Employer Identification Number (EIN) from the IRS (also known as a Federal Tax ID). This number is the equivalent of a Social Security number for a business. It helps the government, banks, and other institutions identify your business. Employers with employees, business partnerships, and corporations and other types of organizations, must obtain an EIN from the IRS. *http://www.irs.gov/*

4. Register with your state and local tax agency. For a complete list of state and local tax authorities: *http://www.business.gov/manage/taxes/state.html*

5. Obtain all the licenses, permits (building permit, vendor license, Department of Health, etc.) and registrations you'll need to start or expand your business. For a complete list by state and locale: *http://business.gov/register/licenses and permits/*

Employment

Employment law can be a minefield that pushes some entrepreneurs to opt for independent contractors and freelancers, as opposed to permanent full-time employees. However, understanding employment law will help you to properly manage employees and ensure that you are protected as the employer.

Independent Contractors vs. Employees

Startups rarely hire full time employees in the first year, but instead hire on an as-needed basis independent contractors and temporary workers, who are referred as 1099's by the IRS (Form 1099 is a form for contractors to report income).

Using independent contractors minimizes the cost of employee benefits, and payroll taxes. However, the IRS looks very closely at 1099's that work exclusively for a company for a long period.

If your independent contractors rely on you for a majority of – or all of – their wages, if they work for you for a long period of time (i.e. a year or more), and if they report to you like normal employees, you may need to convert them to W-2 employees in order to avoid a significant penalty from the IRS.

Hiring Full-Time Employees

If you're thinking of hiring full-time employees, your business must be stable and going pretty well. Before you make an offer to your first employee, review these critical steps to hiring employees to ensure that you are in compliance with key federal and state regulations.

1. **Form SS-4**: Obtain an Employer Identification Number from the IRS (Form SS-4) at www.irs.gov.

2. **Form W-4**: Set up records for withholding taxes. Have employees fill out and sign a Federal Income Tax Withholding Form (W-4) on or before the date of employment. Depending on your state, you may also be required to withhold state taxes, so check your state tax authority.

3. **Form I-9**: Within three days of hire, employers must complete an Employment Eligibility Verification Form, commonly referred to as an I-9 form, and by examining acceptable forms of documentation supplied by the employee, confirm the employee's citizenship and eligibility to work in the United States. This form is not filed with the government, but the employer is required to keep an I-9 form on file for three years after the date of hire or one year after the date the employee's termination, whichever is later.

4. **Register with your state's New Hire Reporting program**: The Personal Responsibility and Work Opportunity Reconciliation Act of 1996 requires all employers to report newly hired and rehired employees to a state directory within 20 days of their hire or rehire date.

5. **Obtain Workers' Compensation Insurance**: Businesses with employees are required to carry Workers' Compensation Insurance coverage through a commercial carrier, on a self-insured basis, or through the state Workers' Compensation Insurance program. Visit your state's Workers' Compensation Office more information on your state's program.

6. **Unemployment Insurance Tax Registration:** Businesses with employees are required to pay unemployment insurance taxes under certain conditions. If your business is required to pay these taxes, you must register your business with your state's workforce agency.

7. **Obtain Disability Insurance (if required):** Some states require employers to provide partial wage replacement insurance coverage to their eligible employees for non-work related sickness or injury. Currently, six states or U.S. territories require that you carry disability insurance: California, Hawaii, New York, New Jersey, Puerto Rico and Rhode Island.

8. **Post required posters and notices:** Employers are required by state and federal laws to prominently display certain posters in the workplace that inform employees of their rights and employer responsibilities under labor laws. These free posters are available from federal and state labor agencies. Visit the Workplace Posters page for specific federal and state posters you'll need for your business

9. **File your taxes:** Generally, each quarter, employers who pay wages subject to income tax withholding, Social Security, and Medicare taxes must file IRS Form 941, Employer's Quarterly Tax Return. Small businesses with an annual income tax liability of $1,000 or less may file IRS Form 944, Employer's Annual Federal Tax Return instead of Form 941. You must also file IRS Form 940, Employer's Annual Federal Unemployment (FUTA) Tax Return, if you paid wages of $1,500 or more in any calendar quarter or you had one or more employees work for you in any 20 or more different weeks of the year.

Employee Handbooks

Before you hire any employees, make sure to create an employee handbook. This handbook should clearly outline all the laws and regulations that your company and your employees must comply with as well as your expectations of them as employees.

Employee handbooks are necessary to protect you as an employer from employee misconduct (such as stealing trade secrets or mistreating other employees) as well as to provide employees with a set of expectations.

1. **Compensation & Benefits**. Explain deductions for federal and state taxes, pay schedules, performance reviews and salary increases, overtime pay, timekeeping, breaks, and bonus compensation. Detail health insurance options, disability insurance, worker's compensation, COBRA, retirement, employee assistance, tuition reimbursement, business travel, and any other fringe benefits.

2. **Work Schedules**. Describe your company's policy regarding work hours and schedules, including attendance, punctuality, reporting absences, flexible schedules and telecommuting.

3. **Standards of Conduct**. Explain how you expect your employees to act, including dress codes and professional conduct. Explain your company's legal and regulatory obligations (for example, to protect customer data, etc).

4. **Anti-Discrimination Policies**. As an employer, you must comply with equal employment opportunity laws and the Americans with Disabilities Act. Your employee handbook should include a section about these laws, and how your employees are expected to comply.

5. **Safety & Security**. Describe your company's policy for creating a safe and secure workplace, including compliance with OSHA laws that require employees to report all accidents, injuries, potential safety hazards, safety suggestions and health and safety related issues to management. Also include security guidelines like physical security policies (locking doors) and information security (protecting computer data).

6. **Media Relations**. Detail how employees should handle calls from reporters. You should have a single point of contact for all media inquiries (you or your PR agency). You don't want your employees speaking about your business in ways that could easily be misrepresented in the media.

7. **Leave**. Family medical leave, jury duty, military leave, time off for court cases, and voting should all be documented to comply with state and local laws. In addition, you should explain your policies for vacation, holiday, bereavement, and sick leave.

8. **Non-Disclosure Agreements and Non-Compete Statements**. While not legal requirements, having employees sign NDAs and conflict of interest statements helps to protect your trade secrets and company proprietary information.

Employment Agreements: Non-disclosure and Non-compete

Any employee who is working on or could come into contact with valuable proprietary company information (such as client lists, business plans, software code, formulas, processes, etc.) should sign a non-disclosure agreement and possibly a non-compete agreement. This could be a separate agreement or a part of a signed employee handbook.

Trade secrets are defined as "anything with independent economic value derived from the fact that it is not widely known or easily obtained." These secrets can include strategic plans, software code, a formula, pattern, compilation, program, device, method, a technique or process, or even recipes that you have made reasonable efforts to keep secret.

Trade secrets differ from other forms of intellectual property such as patents, trademarks and copyrights because they are never registered and never revealed. A confidentiality agreement regarding a trade secret would likely have no end date.

Non-disclosure agreements (or confidentiality agreements) are agreements entered into by two or more parties that protect sensitive information (like trade secrets and other intellectual property) from disclosure to others. When a person signs a non-disclosure agreement, they agree not to share the confidential information with anyone else. These agreements are important in the recording and enforcement of trade secrets and other intellectual property protection such as patents that are pending or in development.

By signing a **non-compete agreement**, an employee promises not
to work for a direct competitor for a specified period of time after
leaving the company.

Non-compete agreements protect your company's confidential
information. If one of your employees has access to sensitive
business information or trade secrets, you'll want to prevent this
employee from disclosing this information to your competitors.

When an employee with access to trade secrets leaves or is fired, he
may open a competing business or go to work for a competitor and
accidentally or deliberately divulge your secrets to success. A
properly drafted non-compete agreement can keep this from
happening.

An astounding percentage of trade secret misappropriations occur
on an employee's last day(s) of work. When parting ways with an
employee, make sure to have steps in place to prevent the copying
of important data. Remind the employee of their non-disclosure
and non-compete agreement and give them a copy. If they did not
read the employee handbook or the agreement they signed on the
first day, they may not remember their obligations.

While non-compete agreements are a very effective way to protect
your trade secrets, the legal system puts a high value on a person's
right to earn a living. Non-compete agreements must:

- Must be reasonable in term and scope (usually no more than
  2 years) and have a good business reason (such as protecting
  your trade secrets and customer base). Most non-competes
  range from six months to two years and are very specific
  with respect to geography or industry and competition.
- Provide some benefit to the employee in exchange for his
  or her promise not to compete against you. Making a job
  offer contingent on signing a non-compete agreement

satisfies this requirement, since the employee is receiving a job in exchange. For existing employees, raises, bonuses, and promotions can also be consideration.

Non-compete agreements are not enforceable against employees in California. However, California employers can use non-solicitation agreements and non-disclosure agreements to protect their trade secrets (client lists, technologies, etc.) when an employee leaves.

Taxes

Financial laws, such as the legislation regarding Capital Gains Tax, can seem daunting when you first become an entrepreneur. The sale of assets and other activities requires a special kind of attention, which is one reason to choose an excellent accountant who will provide good advice.

Income tax

If your entity is taxed at the corporate level (not a pass-through), you will be taxed the corporate income tax rate (15%-35%) and then again at the personal level. If your entity is a pass-through entity such as an LLC, the profits of your business will be taxed at your personal income tax rate (10%-35%). Make sure to calculate income taxes in your financial models and business plan. Set aside taxes as you incur income so that you will be prepared at tax time.

Sales tax

Most companies that sell goods and services have to pay sales tax. Depending on your city and county, this tax can be 5%-10%. Consider opening a second bank account to set aside sales tax so that you're prepared and able to pay at tax time.

Capital gains tax

Gains on the sale of assets (such as stock or real estate) are also taxed. Capital gains tax can be significant when a company has an initial public offering (IPO). A special low capital gains rate is available for stock of C Corps with less than $50 million in gross assets at the time the stock is issued if the corporation is engaged in an active business and if the taxpayer holds the stock for at least five years.

Securities and Raising Capital

When you raise equity capital, you have to comply with securities laws. Securities are regulated by the SEC and by states. States play a big role in regulating securities. Securities laws, deal terms, and their implications are too important and too complex to tackle on your own. When raising capital, hire an attorney that specializes in corporate and securities law, specifically in raising angel and venture capital.

Probably the most important thing to check when you raise capital is that your investors are accredited investors (also referred to as qualified investors).

An accredited investor is defined by the Securities and Exchange Commission (SEC) under Regulation D to refer to investors who are financially sophisticated and have a reduced need for the protection provided by certain government filings.

In order for an individual to qualify as an accredited investor, he or she must accomplish *at least one* of the following:
1. Earn an individual income of more than $200,000 per year, or a joint income of $300,000, in each of the last two years.
2. Have a net worth exceeding $1 million, either individually or jointly with a spouse.
3. Be a general partner, executive officer, or director for the issuer of the security being offered.

There are three basic structures used by angel investors to invest in startups:
1. Convertible Note (debt converts to equity)
2. Preferred Stock (equity with special rights)
3. Common Stock (equity with no special rights)

Angel and venture capital investors rarely invest in a **common stock** structure because it does not give them enough control and security in the deal. Common stock is typical in later rounds of investment when shareholders can be assured that a trustworthy and independent Board of Directors has control of the company and their investment dollars.

Angel and venture investors strongly favor **preferred stock** because it gives them more control over their money. This structure makes sense for most angel or venture capital rounds over $500,000. Preferred stock has additional rights. One of these is usually a *liquidation preference*, meaning that preferred investors get their investment dollars (and return on investment) back before the founders and common shareholders get paid out. This class of stock also usually comes with a Board Seat and protective provisions that give them the right to approve major actions of the company like incurring debt or selling the company.

Convertible notes are more entrepreneur-friendly and are useful for small rounds in the first year or two, when the valuation of the company is anyone's guess. Lawyers often advise entrepreneurs to use convertible notes because startups can't afford the cost of a preferred equity agreement. Legal fees for preferred equity deals can cost between $25,000 and $50,000, so for a small round of investment (under $500,000), the legal fees can be a significant portion of the round.

A convertible note is a form of debt that can be converted into equity (usually preferred) under predetermined circumstances, such as when the note is due, or when the company raises a venture or institutional round – for example, a Series A round from VCs.

A convertible note is also referred to as a *bridge loan* because it's used to "bridge" a company between two funding events – for example, between a friends-and-family round and an institutional (VC) round. In most all cases where a convertible-note structure is used, the assumption is that the startup will soon be raising a round of equity financing that will set a valuation for the company – and that the note will convert to equity at that valuation.

In a convertible-note structure, the investor is a note holder until the note is converted into equity. Since it's a loan rather than an equity investment, there's no need to determine a valuation. The valuation is deferred until the company raises an "A" round, where professional investors come in and establish a value for the company. This is advantageous to pre-revenue startup companies because it gives the entrepreneur more time to prove the value of the company.

Since the company has little or no sales and cash flow during this stage, there's hardly anything to base a valuation on. Therefore, deferring valuation is arguably the main advantage of structuring the deal as a note (debt) rather than stock (equity).

If the company does end up raising a round of equity, the note converts into equity – usually preferred shares at the valuation of that round of equity. If the company does not successfully raise a round of equity, the note does not convert, but is paid back with interest according to the terms of the note. Being a note holder offers a little more security because in the worst-case scenario (i.e. bankruptcy proceedings), debt holders are paid before shareholders.

Raising Equity

Raising equity is time consuming and expensive, so make sure that you raise enough capital for **at least 18-24 months** of operation.

If possible, seek out investors who can offer something more than just money – expertise, strategic partnerships, introductions to new customers, etc.

Start by getting introductions to potential investors through your network (lawyer, accountant, etc.) and follow up with a non-confidential **executive summary** of your business.

Don't reveal confidential details about your technology or business model in your executive summary – just the highlights and the potential of the investment. Once they have indicated that they are interested and would like to see more, have them sign a non-disclosure agreement. This will help protect unfiled patents and trade secrets. Typically, investors want to see a full business plan, a financial model, and investor presentation. It may take six months and several meetings before you see a term sheet.

A **term sheet** is a short, readable document (five to 10 pages) that covers the important terms of a contract. Investors use term sheets to negotiate an investment before the deal is "papered" (fully written out in a long contract) and closed (funded). Once the major terms are agreed to, the investor and the company sign the term sheet and have lawyers draw up the contract.

The major items of a term sheet are:
- The amount of money to invest
- The number of shares
- The valuation of the company
- Any liquidation preference
- Dividends
- Who will be on the Board of Directors
- What happens if the company raises money in the future

Here are things to look out for when raising equity:

- Losing control of your business (management controls)
- Dilution of your personal ownership
- Whether the investment provides enough financing for 18-24 months
- Whether the investors offer benefits beyond the capital provided – for instance, their expertise or network
- Whether the investors have deep pockets and can provide additional larger rounds of capital in the future if needed
- Repurchase of your personal stock in the event of termination or resignation
- Security interests being taken in key assets of the company
- Future potential investment rounds and what that means to the dilution of your ownership
- Financial strength of the company post-investment
- Tax implications of the investment

Here are the things investors will look for:
- If a VC fund, whether your company fits within the fund's investment criteria
- Your company's valuation
- Projected return on investment (a function of your company's projected performance and current valuation)
- The level of risk involved
- Influence and control over management strategy and decision making (i.e. seat on the Board of Directors)
- Liquidity of investment, security interests, and the ability to exit in the event of business failure
- Ability to participate in future rounds if the company meets or exceeds projections
- Rights of first refusal to provide future financing
- Registration rights in the event of a public offering
- Financial strength of the company post-investment
- Tax implications of the investment

Contract Law Basics

Contract laws cover the agreements you have with independent contractors, vendors, customers, employees, and anyone you do business with. Understanding the basics of contract law is essential in order to avoid unnecessary risks.

In order to have a contract, there must first be an *offer*. The offer can be an offer for a good or a service or almost anything else. For example, Carl offers to buy a car from Butch for $500. For the most part, the offer will be along the lines of someone promising to do something, buy something or give up something.

The next step in creating a contract is *acceptance*. For example, Butch replies, "Yes, I will sell you my car for $500." A counter offer is not acceptance, but rather a rejection. If Butch says, "I will sell you my car for $1,000 instead of $500," this is a rejection of the initial offer and becomes a counter offer to Carl. Carl must now choose to accept or reject Butch's counter-offer. If Carl rejects the counter offer, the original offer is no longer on the table.

The third step to create a contract is *consideration*. Consideration means that something of value must be exchanged. The consideration would be receiving the car. Consideration in a contract must be mutual – both parties must receive something of value, but the value does not need to be equal – or even fair. Carl can offer to buy Butch's brand new Ferrari for $500. If Butch accepts, then a contract will be made, even though it's not a fair deal.

In order to have a legal contract, a party must have capacity to contract, the purpose of the contract must be lawful, the form of the contract must be legal, the parties must intend to create a legal relationship, and the parties must consent.

Real Estate

Leasing and buying property is a big decision for a company and the deal terms are many times complex. If you're not familiar with commercial leasing, get a commercial broker.

Retail space and office space is split up into Class A and Class B space. Class A is high end and more expensive. This is appropriate for high-end retail stores and large law firms. Class B space is lower end and less expensive.

Estimating Your Office Space Needs

The typical office has **250 square feet per person** in the office (so 10 people = 2,500 SF). This includes offices, hallways, and conference rooms, but not large community areas. This is not an insignificant expense. At $20/SF/year, this amounts to $50,000 a year.

Estimating the Cost of Space

LoopNet is a free online listing of available commercial properties, including photos, prices, and the maximum square footage available.

Examples of actual commercial lease rates:

Manhattan, NY	Class A Retail $200.00/SF/year
Manhattan, NY	Class A Office $70.00/SF/year
Cincinnati, Ohio	Class A Retail $30.00/SF/year
Cincinnati, Ohio	Class A Office $30.00/SF/year
Cincinnati, Ohio	Class B Office $10.00/SF/year
Boise, Idaho	Class A Retail $20.00/SF/year
Boise, Idaho	Class A Office $20.00/SF/year
Boise, Idaho	Class B Office $10.00/SF/year

Types of Leases

- Gross lease: The landlord pays for insurance, taxes, and repairs. Rent is usually higher with this type of lease because many of these costs are included, but the tenant will pay the same amount each month.

- Single-net lease (Net or N): The tenant (lessee) pays property taxes as well as the base rent. The landlord pays for insurance and repairs.

- Double-net lease (Net-Net or NN): The tenant pays for real estate taxes and building insurance as well as base rent. The landlord pays for utilities and repairs.

- Triple-net lease (NNN): The tenant pays for real estate taxes, building insurance, and maintenance (the three "nets") as well as the base rent. The tenant also pays for repairs and maintenance of any common area.

- Percentage lease: The tenant pays base rent plus a percentage of sales. This is common for retail shopping malls.

Negotiating a Lease

There is no standard set of terms for commercial leases – in fact, negotiating is usually expected. If your local real estate market is struggling, you may be able to get a price break or other concessions like a sizable build-out budget from a landlord. If the market is hot and space is full, it's going to be harder to get concessions on terms.

Here's what you need to find out when negotiating a lease:

- What is the rental rate?
- Does the rental rate escalate over time?
- Who pays for utilities?
- Who pays for insurance?
- Who pays for real estate taxes?
- Who pays for maintenance and repairs?
- Who pays for janitorial?
- Who pays for snow removal and landscaping?
- Is there any Common Area Maintenance (CAM) fee and what does it include?
- What is the minimum lease term?
- Is there an option to renew the lease at the same rate?
- Who will pay for the improvements (interior build-out) of the space (also known as "TA" Tenant Allowances)?
- Do you have to restore the space to the original condition when moving out?
- Are you allowed to sublease the space (in the event that you go out of business)?
- How broad is the permitted use of the space (in the event that you have to sublease)?

Having the landlord pay for build out is one way to finance your overall startup costs – especially if your business is a retail store or restaurant. When a landlord pays to finish the interior space to your specifications (carpet, paint, tile, lighting, counters, kitchen, bathrooms, etc.), they amortize the cost of the build out in the lease, meaning that you pay for the build out over time each month.

If an annual rent increase clause is included in the lease, negotiate to have the landlord to give a one or two year grace period and request a cap on the yearly percentage increase.

Negotiating the length – or *term* – of a lease is very important for startups. Landlords will typically offer better terms for longer leases because it eliminates the expense of re-leasing the property and the expense of vacancy.

Signing a long-term lease is risky for startups because this means that you'll be liable for lease payments even if you go out of business. Shorter leases are less risky for startups.

If you have a great location – or if staying in one location is important (as with retail stores) – try to get a renewal option. If things are going well, you want the ability to renew your lease at the same rate.

Protecting Intellectual Property (IP)

Now that you've invested so much time and energy into developing your product, service, and brand, you should consider protecting your intellectual property (IP). There are four types of intellectual property protection:

1. Copyrights
2. Trademarks
3. Trade Secrets
4. Patents

Companies that invest significantly in the research and development of products and technologies typically protect these investments by using patents. Whether it's a formula for a shampoo, software, a design for an engine, or any other kind of product or technology, there's a chance that it might be patentable as long as it's new and unique.

In many cases, developed works can't be fully or even partially patented. In this case, trade secrets are used to protect these technologies. Trade secrets are an alternative strategy to patents and are successfully used by companies large and small. For instance, Coca-Cola uses trade secrets to protect their recipe for Coke.

Trademarks are used by companies to protect brands, slogans, and other marketing material. Subway restaurant wants to be the only restaurant where you can "Eat Fresh", so it spends millions on advertising campaigns, promoting its trademarked slogan.

Copyrights are used to protect written and graphic works like books, articles, photographs, designs, videos, songs, and software.

Type of Protection	Used to protect	Cost to register	Time to register and issue
Copyright © for registered and unregistered copyrights	Written works like books, articles, and songs, as well as graphic and audio works like designs, photographs, videos, and audio recordings. Software code can also be copyrighted.	**$35** to file	Immediate
Trademark ® for registered trademarks ™ for unregistered trademarks	Brand names, logos, designs, and taglines.	**$325** to file. **$1,000** in attorney fees.	13-18 months
Trade Secret	Technologies, products, processes, methods, designs, formulas – and *anything else* that would give a company an advantage.	**Not registered.** Protected through NDAs, Non-Competes, and secrecy.	Immediate
Patent	Technologies, processes, methods, designs, formulas, and plants.	$150-$500 to file. **$3,000-$35,000** in attorney fees.	2-6 years

Length of protection	Cost to litigate	Tips	Registering agency
75 years after author's death	**Minimal.** Damages are clearly defined by law and the courts deal with these cases quickly. Infringers pay damages and attorney fees.	Copyright everything you create. If you hire an independent contractor like a writer, designer or web developer, have them assign the copyrights to you in your contract with them.	Library of Congress and US Patent & Trademark Office (USPTO)
Indefinite as long as fees are paid and mark is in commercial use.	**Significant**	Trademark your brand name, logo, and tagline.	US Patent & Trademark Office (USPTO)
Indefinite as long as company protects the works.	**Significant**	Keep all valuable proprietary technologies and processes confidential within your company. Have any employee who comes into contact with secrets sign an NDA and Non-Compete first. You have up to one year to decide whether to file a patent.	Not registered. Tracked and documented internally by the company.
15-20 years	**Very significant**	Only patent things that have high commercial value, otherwise it's not worth the expense. Most patent applications are not granted.	US Patent & Trademark Office (USPTO)

Copyrights

- Copyrights last 75 years after the author's death. In a sense, they are the **longest, cheapest, and most straightforward form of intellectual property protection**.

- **Put a © on everything** that you create and don't want copied by your competitors.

- A simple " © Copyright *Name Year*" is enough to deter people from stealing your works, but in order to collect damages, you will need to file each work with the USPTO for **$35**.

- **Register your copyrighted works before you think they may be stolen**, but only register those things that would cause you damages (they should have paid for use). You can only get damages from the date you've filed your copyright onward.

- **Get a written assignment of copyright from all independent contractors** (designers, writers, software developers, and other contractors) you hire to create works for you. Employees (W2) are implicit in their copyright assignments, but contractors and consultants are not. Just write in the contract agreement something to the effect of "Contractor assigns copyright of these works to the company".

- Register your copyrights yourself. To make sure you are registering correctly on www.uspto.gov and through the Library of Congress, make an appointment with your attorney's office – a legal assistant or paralegal should be able to show you how to go through the process yourself.

Copyrights

A copyright protects the tangible form of an artist's expression (visual, audio, physical, etc.) from being copied. Protection begins immediately and lasts for the individual artist's life plus 75 years after their death (or 120 years after creation for works-made-for-hire).

Examples of copyrightable works:
- Literary works
- Musical works
- Dramatic works
- Pantomimes and choreographic works
- Pictorial, graphic and sculptural works
- Motion pictures and other audiovisual works
- Sound recordings
- Architectural works
- Computer programs
- Compilations of works
- Derivative works

Companies typically automatically own copyrightable works of employees. However, this is not true of independent contractors.

In order to ensure that you own the copyright of something that you hired someone to create for you (for instance, a logo design, a website, or a written report), you must have them sign a document (either a separate agreement or as a term outlined in your contract) stating that they assign the copyrights to you.

In order to sue someone for copyright infringement, the copyright must be registered. The main benefit to registering a copyright is that it gives you the ability to collect *statutory* damages (predefined damages).

Statutory damages are advantageous because the court can award damages to the copyright owner even if the copyright owner cannot prove that they have been harmed by the infringement – they only need to prove that there's been an infringement.

Statutory damages can range from $750 to $30,000 per infringement, depending upon what the court considers just. If the infringement was willful, statutory damages can go as high as $150,000 per infringement. If the infringement was innocent, the statutory damages can be as low as $200 per infringement.

Trademarks

- **Trademarks last indefinitely** as long as they are maintained both by being used in commerce and with periodic fees (six years, $600; 10 years, $300; and so on). They are more expensive than copyrights and less expensive than patents.

- **Put a ™ on your logo, tagline, and other unique identifiers** that you create and don't want copied by your competitors.

- A simple ™ is enough to deter people from stealing your logo, etc, but **in order to collect damages, you need to register ® your trademark** or service mark with the USPTO for **$325** for each service or class. Attorneys' fees are usually around **$1,000** in addition to the filing fee.

- You can only use the ® symbol after your trademark is issued, which can take **13-18 months**.

- A trademark provides you with **nationwide coverage**.

- Before you settle on a company name or logo, check the USTPO database of Trademarks (TESS) to make sure that there aren't any other companies in your same category (for instance, restaurants or toys) who have a registered trademark. You can do a quick **search** at **www.uspto.gov.**

Trademarks

A trademark is word, slogan, or logo that is used as an identifier of a source of goods or services. Trademarks for services are sometimes called service marks but there is no legal difference.

The purpose of trademarks is to protect the consumer from being confused by companies with similar names or misled by knock-offs.

There are six basic types of trademarks:

1. **Fanciful marks** are words that never existed in the English language prior to use as a trademark – for example, *Exxon* and *KODAK*. These are the strongest form of trademark.

2. **Arbitrary marks** are words that existed in the English language but were associated with completely different things than the goods or services on which the mark is applied – for example, *Apple* for computers and *Domino's* for pizza. These are also a very strong form of trademark.

3. **Suggestive marks** are words that suggest the product or service or suggest an aspect of the product or service on which the mark is applied. Examples: *Whirlpool* for washing machines and *Coppertone* for suntan lotion. These are not as strong as fanciful or arbitrary marks, but are typically protectable as trademarks.

4. **Descriptive marks** are words that describe the product or service on which the mark is applied. Examples: *Honey Roasted Peanuts* or *Vision Center*. Usually not protectable as a mark unless the applicant can prove that the consumer closely associates that mark with the company.

5. **Slogans or Taglines** are protectable as trademarks as long as they are not too descriptive or generic – for example, *Don't leave home without it.*

6. **Logo designs** are typically very strong trademarks.

Trade names (such as those company names registered with the state) are not the same as trademarks and do not provide trademark protection.

Trademark notice with a ™ is advisable but not necessary. Use TM for unregistered trademarks or SM for unregistered service marks. Use ® for registered trademarks and service marks.

There are several types of marks that cannot be protected as trademarks, including generic words or phrases, marks confusingly similar to existing trademarks, and marks that become so ubiquitous with the English language that they lose distinctiveness and become generic (for example, *aspirin, escalator,* and *yo-yo*).

Trademarks are protected under common law. Under state and federal law, protection begins immediately upon one's use of the mark in commerce as a trademark. Much stronger protection is available though federal registration of a trademark with the USPTO.

You can apply for federal registration before using the mark. A registered trademark ® provides nationwide protection without necessitating nationwide use. Registered trademarks are easier to enforce in federal courts than unregistered trademarks (and easier to collect damages), and are therefore more likely to be avoided by competitors.

Before you invest any money in a product name, company name, product packaging, or advertising campaign, do a **trademark availability search** first either by hiring an attorney or by using the TESS search engine at uspto.gov. Make sure that your proposed mark is not confusingly similar to existing marks. This will ensure that you are not infringing on anyone else's mark and also that your mark is available to register.

A key question in the trademark disputes is whether a consumer of products or services under an existing mark could be confused by the intended use of the proposed mark. Examiners will look at the similarity of the proposed and the existing marks themselves and the similarity of the products and services being offered.

Filing a Trademark

Most applicants file electronically using the USPTO's Trademark Application System (TEAS). The application fee is $325 per mark and per classification.

Examination usually takes six months to a year. The examiner will reject the application if they believe that the mark is too descriptive or is confusingly similar to an existing mark. If the examiner rejects the mark, the applicant can respond with an argument. If the mark is allowed, the USPTO publishes the mark for thirty days on the Federal Register, thus making it available for opposition. If unopposed, the mark issues shortly after.

Trade Secrets

- **Trade Secrets last indefinitely** as long as they are never disclosed. Some of the largest and most successful companies in the world use trade secrets to protect their intellectual property instead of patents to protect their unique know-how. Coca-Cola uses trade secrets to protect the formulation of Coke.

- **Trade Secrets do not have an external costs (like filing fees)**, but instead the cost is in the process of keeping company secrets a secret and making sure employees, competitors, and others never steal or gain access to the whole process.

- Until you decide whether to patent something or keep it a trade secret, make sure to document your processes, but keep them confidential and only disclose them to employees on a need-to-know basis.

- A simple **employee confidentiality agreement, non-compete, and trade secret agreement** is enough to deter employees from stealing your intellectual property, but in order to sleep well at night, **try to keep any one employee from gaining access to all aspects of your trade secret(s)**.

- In order to prove that something is a trade secret, you must show active steps to maintain secrecy.

Trade Secrets

A trade secret is information that derives independent economic value (actual or potential) from not being generally known or readily ascertainable by others who could benefit from its disclosure (such as competitors, customers, and vendors). Trade secrets are partially defined by the efforts that are taken to maintain their secrecy.

There is no presumption of a trade secret. The owner must show active steps to maintain its secrecy, for example:
1. identify the trade secret in a record **(lock it up)**
2. limit knowledge to those having **need to know**
3. establish, document and follow a **trade secret policy**
4. wisely use **confidentiality, non-compete, non-disclosure** and **non-solicitation agreements**

Any type of information that meets these criteria above could be trade secrets. Typical types of trade secrets include scientific or **technical information** such as designs, processes, procedures, formulas, patterns, compilations, programs, devices, methods, techniques or improvements as well as **business information** such as financial information, listing of names, addresses or telephone numbers, marketing plans, business strategies, and business policies.

An astounding percentage of trade secret misappropriations occur on an **employee's last day(s) of work.** Trade secret misappropriations are commonly enforced under state law, but in egregious circumstances, a trade secret misappropriation can be enforced by a federal prosecutor under the Economic Espionage Act of 1996.

Patents

- Patents are the **most expensive form of intellectual property protection** to file and to enforce.

- A non-provisional patent (fully filed official patent application) can cost anywhere from **$3,500 to $35,000** to file with an attorney.

- **65%-70% of patent applications are rejected.** Working with an attorney to determine patentability and prepare the application improves your odds.

- A fully filed non-provisional patent application takes **two to six years to issue.**

- A patent provides you with nationwide coverage, but in order to get international protection, you'll need additional filings in other countries (PCT, etc).

- Before you develop something, **make sure someone else hasn't patented it**. Search the USTPO database of patents for similar products or companies with issued and active patents in your field.

- If your only goal is to be able to put "Patent Pending" on your product, website, or materials, but you're not sure that you have a $10 million product (or that you're willing to go the distance on a full patent), **file a Provisional Patent yourself for $125**. A provisional patent is a rough draft that lasts for 12 months and does not protect you from infringement or enable you to collect damages.

- **Talk to a patent attorney** about your options before you make any serious decisions (such as filing a provisional yourself).

Patents

The purpose of patents is to accelerate innovation. To do this, the government grants a limited monopoly to the inventor in exchange for the inventor's complete public disclosure how to make and use the technology.

Patents last anywhere from 14 years for a design patent (how does it look) to 20 years for a utility patent (how does it work).

Patents are the most expensive form of intellectual property protection to file and to litigate. On average it takes **six years** to get a patent successfully issued. The average out-of-pocket **cost for a patent is $35,000**.

For technology-based startups, patents can be strategic assets in the financing process – increasing the pre-money valuation of the company and the bargaining position of the founders.

However, the high cost of filing patent applications and the high cost of enforcing issued patents deters many startups from filing them – instead, either copyrighting software code or protecting their intellectual property with trade secrets.

Before pursuing a patent-protection strategy, startups should consider:

1. How easy it is for competitors to design around the potential patent.
2. Whether the technology is actually patentable and how well the claims would stand up in court.
3. Whether disclosing the secrets in a patent is preferred to relying on trade secrets.

A provisional patent (12 month rough draft, *no protection – not a complete application*) can cost **$125** to file on your own and a non-provisional patent (fully filed official patent application) can cost anywhere from **$3,500 to $35,000** to file with an attorney. If the patent issues, periodic maintenance fees are required (**$100 - $5,000**) and are due three, seven, and 11 years after the patent is issued.

Between **65% and 70% of patent applications are rejected**. Working with an attorney to determine patentability and prepare the patent application improves your odds, but remember: This is a business for them.

Interestingly, having a patent does not necessarily give you the right to manufacture or sell your product or technology – or *freedom to operate*. Incremental improvements to existing patented technologies or processes are viewed as separate – only the *improvement* is patented – not the whole.

For example, if you patented a table with eight legs, improving on the existing patented four-legged table, you do not have the right to manufacture and sell eight-legged tables. If you did, you would be infringing on the four-legged table patent. In order to market your eight-legged table, you would need to secure a license (or permission) from the four-legged table patent owner.

To avoid spending thousands on patents and prototypes only to find that you're inadvertently infringing on others' patents, do a search for existing patents on USPTO.gov. To be completely sure, have your patent attorney do a search and provide you with a freedom-to-operate opinion.

It can cost more than $1 million in legal fees to sue someone for patent infringement. The bottom line: A patent is a sword, not a shield – and they are only a good investment to the extent that the benefit of protection far exceeds the cost of litigation (i.e., you are protecting your $10 million business or product).

If your business is niche or does not otherwise have the potential to grow revenue over $10 million, a full patent may be a waste of money. Self-filed or attorney-filed provisional patents may serve as cheap deterrents for 12 months until you prove your concept.

There are three types of patents: utility patents, design patents and plant patents. Utility patents are the most common.

1. A **utility patent** is a patent on a functional invention (for example, a new type of bottle opener)
2. A **design patent** is a patent on a non-functional, ornamental design for a product (for example, a design for a Nike shoe)
3. A **plant patent** is a patent on an asexually reproduced, distinct and new variety of a plant (for example, a new pesticide-resistant tomato)

A utility patent is a limited monopoly provided by federal statute (and guaranteed by the U.S. Constitution) giving the patent-holder the right to exclude others from making, using, selling, importing and offering the invention for sale in the United States during the term of the patent.

Patents are enforceable only within the territory of the government that granted the patent (e.g., U.S. patents are only enforceable in the U.S.). For patent protection outside of the United States, the invention needs to be patented separately in every country in which protection is sought. These fees can be significant.

Utility patents can include such inventions as:
- Apparatuses
- Machines

- Articles of manufacture
- Compositions
- Formulas
- Processes
- Software
- Business Methods (in limited circumstances)
- Any improvements to the above

Utility patents have strict patentability requirements. The technology must be **new, novel, and not obvious**.

The patent application must include a disclosure enabling a hypothetical person of ordinary skill in the technology to make and use the invention.

Only the true inventor(s) may apply for the patent – this requirement is called *inventorship*. Inventorship is a legal determination controlled by the Patent Statute: "The formation in the mind of the inventor of a definite and permanent idea of the complete and operative invention as it is thereafter applied in practice."

Patents can have more than one inventor (joint inventorship). To be a joint inventor a person must contribute in some significant manner to *at least one claim* of the patent.

Merely constructing or building a device or system according to another's specific instructions, performing tests on or for an invented device, system or process, explaining to the inventors well-known concepts or the current state of the art, or supervising the work of the inventors does not amount to inventorship.

Patents are initially owned by the inventor; for a company to own the patent, the inventor must assign the invention/patent to the company by written agreement/assignment. There is no work-for-hire doctrine in patents, so employees must specifically assign the rights of a patent to their company in each instance.

Applying for a Utility Patent

Preparation of a patent application must include:
- A detailed description of how to make and use the invention, which must refer to drawings of the invention if drawings may assist in visualizing the invention or its components
- At least one claim defining with particularity the scope of what is being protected (analogous to the property definition on a property deed)
- A declaration signed by the inventor(s)

Provisional patent applications are essentially "informal patent applications" (the statutory requirements are significantly lessened). Cost for preparing is, likewise, usually significantly less (e.g., many provisional applications can be prepared for less than $3,000 by an attorney and the filing fees are $150 for small businesses).

Provisional patent applications are never examined, never issued into a patent and stay pending only for one year. The applicant gets a serial number and filing date from the Patent Office and has 12 months to be completed with a non-provisional filing. Within that one year, the applicant can convert the provisional application into a formal patent application and can claim the benefit of the provisional application's filing date.

Provisional applications provide several advantages. They can be prepared and filed very quickly and inexpensively (compared to formal patent applications) and they allow the applicant to beat competitors to the Patent Office.

The one-year pendency window allows the applicant to consider if the invention will work, if people will buy it, if the invention is patentable, and if it's worth the extra money to pursue a formal patent application.

The **patent time clock** starts when an invention is **published** (in an article or advertisement), **put on sale or sold**, or is put into **public or commercial use**. The inventor has **12 months to submit an application**, or they lose the right to patent the invention. One exception to this 12-month rule is if the invention's public or commercial use is purely experimental.

"Patent Pending" means that a formal or provisional patent application has been filed and that it is still pending (alive) within the Patent Office. It is illegal to falsely use the Patent Pending notice.

Marking products with the patent numbers of issued patents is not required but is highly recommended. This allows patent damages to accrue immediately upon infringement – otherwise damages start accruing only after the patent holder puts the infringer on formal notice of the patent and the infringement.

Do Your Own Patent Research

If you're considering patenting an invention, find out whether your innovation has already been patented. The U.S. Patent and Trademark Office has patents and trademarks on a searchable database at www.uspto.gov.

Talk to a patent attorney to find out whether they believe your innovation fits the criteria of patentability, how much they might charge for a patent, and how friendly they could be with your bill. If you can't afford the fees and can't find a patent attorney willing to reduce their fee or postpone their bill, you might consider filing a provisional patent on your own. The filing fee for a small business for a provisional patent online at www.uspto.gov is $150.

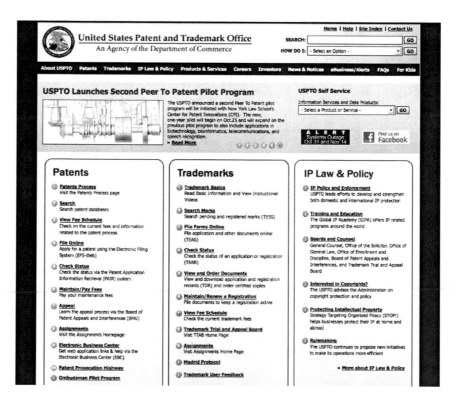

Product Liability

Defective or dangerous products cause of thousands of injuries every year in the U.S. Manufacturers and sellers can be held liable for selling a defective product to a consumer.

Responsibility for a product defect that causes injury lies with everyone in the distribution chain – including the manufacturer, a manufacturer of component parts, the wholesaler, and the retail store that sold the product to the consumer.

The law requires that products meet the "ordinary expectations" of consumers. When a product has an unexpected defect or danger – or causes unexpected injury – it does not meet the ordinary expectations of consumers.

There are **three types of product defects: design defects, manufacturing defects, and marketing defects.** Design defects are present in a product from the beginning, even before it is manufactured, in that something in the design of the product is inherently unsafe. Manufacturing defects are those that occur in the course of a product's manufacture or assembly. Marketing defects are flaws in the way a product is marketed, such as improper labeling, insufficient instructions, or inadequate safety warnings.

By their nature, some products simply cannot be made safer without losing their usefulness – these are *unavoidably unsafe products*. For example, a knife that is too dull to injure anyone would be useless for its intended use of cutting food.

Manufacturers and suppliers of unavoidably unsafe products must give proper warnings of the dangers and risks of their products so that consumers can make informed decisions about whether to use them.

Business Insurance

Business insurance protects your investment in your business by minimizing financial risks associated with unexpected events such as a death of a partner, an injured employee, a lawsuit, or a natural disaster.

Business insurance is not required for every business, but most businesses carry insurance. Startups that are still nascent (not yet shipping product, serving customers, opening locations or physical offices) may not need insurance. However, once product is shipping or locations are opened, insurance is necessary.

Your state, lender, or investors may require specific types of business insurance.

Types of Business Insurance

- General Liability Insurance – a catch-all sort of insurance that covers legal hassles due to accident, injuries, and negligence claims. General liability insurance starts out at about $500 per year for a $1 million policy.
- Product Liability Insurance – covers companies that manufacture, wholesale, distribute, and sell products.
- Professional Liability Insurance - protects your business against malpractice, errors, and negligence claims.
- Commercial Property Insurance - covers everything related to the loss or damage of company property due to fire, flood, etc.

First, **assess your risks**. Do you have employees? Do you have a store or office where someone could get hurt? Could someone get hurt from using your product? Could someone sue you for malpractice? Do you have key partners or employees? Do you have important assets that could be destroyed by fire, flood, tornado, or other natural disasters?

Find a reputable, licensed insurance broker who specializes in businesses. Talk about your needs and determine what type of coverage is best for you.

Shop around and assess your insurance coverage annually. As your business grows, so do your liabilities.

There are several **factors that will affect your premium** (the cost of insurance):

- How many business locations do you have?
- Do you have a home office, own location, lease location?
- How many employees do you have?
- How many vehicles do you have?
- What is the total annual sales and annual payroll for your business?
- How is your business registered? (LLC, C Corp, S Corp, etc)
- How old is your business?
- What is the total square footage that your business occupies?
- How much would it cost to replace your business personal property at your business location?
- How old/new is the property, its sprinklers & alarms systems, etc.?

Get Quotes on Insurance

InsuranceEdge.com offers quotes from the major business insurance providers, including general liability, business property, workers' compensation, commercial auto, and umbrella coverage.

10   Two Business Plans

The best preparation for tomorrow is to do today's work superbly well.

— *Sir William Osler*

Whether you're applying for a loan or pitching to venture capital or angel investors, you're going to need a solid business plan. Business plans are required to convince lenders and investors that the proposed business is sound — and to clearly detail all of the things that need to happen in order for the business to be successful.

Even if you're not planning on raising outside financing, a business plan is still absolutely essential. It doesn't need to be fancy, but it does need to cover the major points in the business model and feasibility chapters of this book.

Business Plan for Investors & Lenders
(adapted from Sequoia Capital)

- **Company Purpose**
  - o Define the business in a single declarative sentence.

- **Problem**
  - o Describe the pain of the customer (or the customer's customer). Outline how the customer addresses the issue today.

- **Solution**
  - o Demonstrate your company's value proposition to make the customer's life better.
  - o Show where your product physically sits. Provide use cases.

- **Why Now**
  - o Set up the historical evolution of your category. Define recent trends that make your solution possible.

- **Market Size**
  - o Identify and profile the customer you will cater to. Calculate the total addressable market (TAM) from the top down.
  - o Calculate the SAM and SOM (Serviceable Addressable Market and Serviceable Obtainable Market) from the bottoms up.

- **Competition**
  - o List all your competitors and their competitive advantages.
  - o List your competitive advantages.

- **Product**
  - o Describe your product or service (functionality, features, intellectual property, etc).
  - o Outline your product roadmap – how will the product develop in the future?

- **Business Model**
  - o Define your revenue model – how do you make money? Outline your pricing structure and how it compares to your competitors or to the alternative.
  - o What is the average account size or lifetime value of a customer?
  - o Describe your sales and distribution model. How will customers find and purchase your product?
  - o List all your potential customers and show what your sales pipeline could look like over the next 24 months.

- **Team**
  - o Describe the founders and management team. What skills or connections do they possess that will make the business successful?
  - o Describe your current and potential advisers and mentors.

- **Pro Forma Financials**
  - o P&L
  - o Balance sheet
  - o Cash flow (24 months)
  - o Capitalization table
  - o Valuation and deal terms (if raising money from investors)
  - o Personal financial statement (if applying for a loan)

Checklist for the Entrepreneur

- **Organize personal finances**
  - o Evaluate personal balance sheet
  - o Track spending
  - o Monitor credit score
  - o Cut personal expenses

- **Sketch out business model**

- **Calculate feasibility**
  - o Calculate unit profitability
  - o Calculate operating profitability
  - o Calculate investment profitability
    - ▪ Calculate startup expenses
  - o Research market size
  - o Get customer feedback
  - o Build Profit & Loss and Cash Flow pro forma financial models

- **Evaluate financing options (debt versus equity)**
  - o Research local SBA lenders
  - o Research local angel investors

- **Create a brand**
  - o Research target customers
  - o Research competitors and alternatives
  - o Brainstorm the brand with five creative friends
    - ▪ Brand attributes & values
    - ▪ Name options
    - ▪ Tagline options
  - o Search domain name & trademark availability
  - o Create design brief for designers
  - o Crowdsource logo & website designs

- **Create a marketing & publicity plan**
  - Create press releases & publicity plan
  - Create an advertising budget
  - Crowdsource ad designs
  - Create social media plan
  - Create viral marketing plan
  - Create email newsletters
  - Create search engine optimization strategy

- **Set up back office operations**
  - Create website
  - Set up email
  - Set up voicemail
  - Set up project management forums
  - Set up accounting system
  - Prepare tax return

- **Legal**
  - Create a separate legal entity (if desired) and file necessary forms with the IRS and state
  - File trademark application for name, tagline, & logo
  - File copyrights on website copy and other materials
  - Protect technologies, processes, etc with patents and/or trade secrets
  - Get copyright assignments from independent contractors (designers, web developers, etc)
  - Have employees sign non-disclosure and non-compete agreements
  - Create an employee handbook and file necessary forms with the IRS and state before hiring employees
  - Set aside funds for income, sales, and other applicable taxes

Acknowledgements

First, I must thank Steve Boord for being a wonderful mentor and teacher. You opened doors and taught me almost everything I know. Thank you.

Carolyn Pione Micheli, you are the best colleague, friend, and advocate a girl could have. Thank you for all your wisdom and support.

To Tom Neyer – thank you for giving me a dream job that I will never forget.

Bill Cunningham, your relentless optimism and can-do attitude are inspiring. Thank you for believing in me and dreaming big.

To Eric Avner for supporting nearly everything I've done – literally and figuratively. Thank you. You're the absolute best and I don't know what we'd do without you.

To James Zimmerman, CincyTech, Taft Stettinius & Hollister, the Cincinnati Chamber, and all of the supporters of Cincinnati Innovates – you've made it possible for me to work with truly extraordinary people.

To all the folks who pitch in to pull off death-defying feats like InOneWeekend (and smile all the way) – sincere thanks. And special thanks to Roy Gilbert and Ali Rowghani for flying thousands of miles to inspire so many entrepreneurs.

To Rahul Mehendale, Diana O'Brien, Ken Hutt, Ruben Gavieres, Charlie Hill, Anupam Narula, Betosini Chakraborthy, Bobby Moss, Christian Mazzi, Neal Batra, Denzil Wilson, Steve Atkins, Gabriel Chenevoy, Sachin Palod, Payal Kadakia Pande, Sanjay Behl, and Richard Palmer, and all my Deloitte Strategy & Operations friends – it was a truly exceptional experience to work with you. Rahul, you were the only person who ever told me that I needed to "work harder or I wouldn't cut it around here." Thank you. I needed that.

Proofreading and editing the content of this book was no small feat. Thank you, Nikki Kingery, for your dedication.

To Molly Sandquist, Amber Burke Sprengard, Chris Bollman, Adam Paulisick, Jeff Stamp, David Willbrand, Debbie Edwards, Michael Bergman, Bob Bonder, Andrew Paradies, Brad King, Charles Matthews, Dov Rosenberg, Colleen Post, Joe Pantuso, Chris Ostoich, Dave Knox, JB Kropp, Krista Neher, Josh Fendley, Margaret Lawson, George Molinski, Kevin Dugan, Joshua Johnson, Tammy Riddle, Stephen Samuels, Keara Schwartz, Chaz Giles, William Dickson, Jeff Nabors, Anna Berding Singh, Ken Bloemer, Paul Brinker, Larry Bell, Greg Verderber, Michelle Spelman, Jon Schlinkert, Jeff Spelman, Karl Perron, Jason Heikenfeld, Bob Coy, Mike Venerable, Justin Thompson, Dorothy Air, Pat Longo, Bob Baron, Dan O'Keeffe, Joe Sprengard, Dacia Snider, Kevin Kirsch, David Mancino, Clint Nelsen, Tony Shipley, Jim Cunningham, Pat McBride, Chris Rose, Carol Frankenstein, Ali Malekzadeh, Joe Carter, Mark Richey, Rob Heimann, Maribeth Rahe, Rich Kiley, Larry Huston, Phil Collins, Drew Boyd, Tim Schigel, and Pete Blackshaw, for the education, the inspiration, and the open doors. Without you, I wouldn't have anything to write about. Thank you.

Sincere thanks to my talented graduate and undergraduate interns who researched topics for this book over the summer – Suprasanna Mishra, Chad Eckerlin, Matt Anthony, Amanda Starnes, Kathleen Kinnemeyer, Patrick Mouch, Miguel Rueda, Galia Hyun, and Ekaterina Hines. I know you will graduate to go on to far higher pursuits. Don't get a job – start a company.

To Peter for being a good sport and sounding board these last few months. Thank you for all the love and support. And to Carrie – thank you for all the encouragement. You are a living example of kindness.

And last, but certainly not least – to my mom, Patricia, and my family – thank you for loving me and cheering me on. Mom, thank you for setting the bar high and loving me unconditionally. I am so lucky to have you.

In memory of John Krekeler and Tracey Edwards. You are always missed.

Index

About the Author

Elizabeth Edwards launched Metro Innovation, a catalyst for innovation and entrepreneurship, in 2009 after seven years in venture capital, private equity, and strategy and innovation consulting.

As a venture capital investor at Neyer Holdings, Edwards built winning strategies for start-up and growth companies in a variety of sectors, including clean tech, life sciences, consumer products, and technology. She has evaluated hundreds of business plans, and actively participated in the funding, launch, and management of five early stage portfolio companies.

Edwards started her career at Deloitte Consulting, where she was a strategy consultant to Fortune 500 companies, deployed over a broad range of industries. At Deloitte, Edwards' work focused on strategic marketing, disruptive innovation, and growth strategies.

Edwards holds a B.S. in Economics and Cognitive Psychology from the University of Michigan, where she graduated with honors and distinction, and a MBA from the University of Cincinnati.

She is a resident of Cincinnati, Ohio, where she serves on the board of the Greater Cincinnati Venture Association and teaches Entrepreneurial Finance at Xavier University.

She has been featured in more than 50 local and national media outlets, including the *Wall Street Journal* and *BoingBoing*, and has been a popular guest lecturer at universities and conferences since 2007, where she presents entrepreneurship as an imperative for economic stability.

Follow along @eedwards

Additional templates and downloads are available at
www.elizabethedwards.com

CPSIA information can be obtained at www.ICGtesting.com
262229BV00002B/55/P